Fraser J. Hay

How to Make Money on Ecademy

© Fraser J. Hay

ISBN 1-905823-01-0

9 781905 823017

Book layout design and setting: Jaquetta Trueman
Book text set in 11pt Myriad Pro Regular

First published in 2006 by Ecademy Press

Contact:
Ecademy Press
6, Woodland Rise
Penryn, Cornwall, UK
TR10 8QD

info@ecademy-press.com

Printed and Bound by Lightning Source UK and USA

Some interesting facts

- I joined Ecademy.com on 6th July, 2005
- I created 20 people in my network within 8 hours and had to upgrade
- Within a day, I had generated 45 new prospects for my wares
- Within a week I was generating £50 extra profit per day
- Within a month, I was testing lots of new approaches, learning daily
- Within 2 months, I had created 2 new sources of revenue via Ecademy
- Within 3 months, My average sales transaction value had risen by 125%
- Within 4 months, I had increased my extra profit by as much as £200 a day.
- Within 5 months, I had increased my extra profit by as much as £1000 in a single day.
- Within 6 months, I had increased my extra profit by as much as £5000 in a single day.
- … and it's getting better and better and better.

Will you be able to do the same? Well, one thing's for sure, there's no reason why not. Everything I've done and how I've done it, is in here. The rest, as they say … is up to you.

You just don't know how big this is going to get.

Yours sincerely

Fraser J. Hay

Fraser J. Hay

Contents

PART ONE: A Crash Course in Networking

PART TWO: Where Business People Click

Acknowledgements

The author would like to thank the following people for helping in the creation of this book, and supporting material.

Mindy Gibbins-Klein & Andy Coote of Ecademy Press, who attended my first ever "Quantum profits" workshop, and encouraged me to publish this book.

Martin Shepherdly, who produced the first video of one of my live sessions

Jaquetta Trueman, typesetter, designer and editor who patiently put up with me, during the whole publishing process.

Stewart Chalmers, Stephen Harvard Davis, and Simon Phillips, who patiently mentor me, and listen to my mad ravings, mumblings and ideas.

Thomas Power (Yoda), who shared numerous phone calls, meetings and emails with me, offering his 100% support, encouragement and contacts.

Jon Game for his assistance in co-creating the How to Make Money on Ecademy Companion tool.

Phillip Banks, voiceover extraordinaire, for his time, commitment and sheer professionalism in the production of the audio material.

The many "Blackstars" on Ecademy, who have offered the benefit of their knowledge, experience and support, and who many have now become good friends.

The hundreds of Red Hand Gang members and fellow ecademists for their testimonials, emails, letters, phone calls and SMS of encouragement and support.

And finally my wife, Wendy for all her courage, support and for putting up with all my nonsense.

PART ONE

A Crash Course in Networking

My Formula for Networking

E   Educate yourself about your needs and the needs of others

C   Characters and personality styles in Networking

A   Arouse interest in others with a great Elevator pitch

D   Do's & Don'ts of Developing Relationships when Networking

E   Engage, Enthuse & Encourage those in your network

M   Motivate yourself, maintain momentum & make it happen

Y   Your objectives and progress re-visited

What is Networking?

One definition of networking is perhaps meeting someone new for the first time with a view to exploring possible mutual opportunities, and the possibility of developing a relationship.

Here are some more definitions of networking:

"People caring about People"

"What goes around, comes around"

"An organised way of creating links and opportunities with, and for people"

"Giving and contributing to others, and asking nothing in return"

With Ecademy.com, you will discover how networking can actually mean a whole lot more and can become an acquired skill for both social and commercial settings.

Turn each page slowly, and absorb the hints, tips, and powerful techniques I am going to share with you, but most importantly, at the end of each section I have included my personal checklist for you to run through and confirm that you are indeed putting it all into practice and proving my techniques can and do work for you and your business too.

Remember, I can lead a horse to water …

The way it used to be

Traditionally, individuals would network, swap business cards, or meet old and new acquaintances at the following places:-

- Chambers of Commerce
- Exhibition
- Trade show
- Business club
- Business Link, local enterprise company
- A networking event

As you will discover in Part 2 of this book, Ecademy.com uses a 'referrals only' approach to attract elite groups of business minded individuals, that can all help you to promote you, your business, your products and services, and even find employment, and suppliers – you name it.

Ecademy is the largest networking community site in the UK, currently with over 74,000 members (and expanding rapidly in the USA) enabling individuals to share contacts, experiences, knowledge and expertise. One of the major paradigm shifts in doing business in the 21st century and doing business online, especially when it comes to Ecademy – is to SHARE.

- Share your knowledge
- Share your expertise
- Share your contacts
- Share your skills

The whole ethos of Ecademy is all about sharing.

The more you share, the more people will want to recommend you, to others. Referral rates of over 25% have been reported by members. There is a high referral rate, because people's personal networks begin to overlap, and people very quickly begin to recognise and know mutual acquaintances who could benefit from the services offered by a particular individual.

If that person is well known and liked, then the word of mouth, or word of mouse will spread even quicker, increasing their awareness and exposure within the business network on the site.

Professionals from hundreds of industries are actively searching the extended networks of their trusted business contacts on Ecademy to discover inside connections to potential business partners, to get in touch with industry experts for advice, or to find recommended professionals to fill open job positions, or fulfill contracts.

Did you know …

- Approximately 80% of all jobs are never advertised, and are filled via networking

- The average person knows about 200-250 people with whom you can connect

- Anyone in the world that you might want to meet is only five or six personal introductions away

- That 90% of people don't have a business card

Networking Principle #1

 ## Educate yourself about your needs and the needs of others

Whether it's to find a job, find a supplier, find customers, joint venture partners, find referrals or simply to make friends, you first need to educate yourself about your needs and the needs of others. Let's look at several key factors that you will also have to consider if you want to succeed in networking.

You need to think about your mindset, temperament and/ or disposition with regards to networking, what you want to achieve from your networking endeavours, and what you can offer the individuals and organisations you will encounter on your networking journey. Many people fear rejection, obligation, appearing too pushy, or in some occasions, appearing too weak, and each of these issues need to be addressed and overcome.

Therefore, it's very likely that the mindset of the majority of people in networking may actually be hindering the development of their personal networks. So one of the first things, you should consider is adopting the right mindset.

Mindset for Success

Do not let fear get in your way. Many people are afraid of meeting new people, selling or presenting in front of others. If you have never been involved in any sort of networking before, you will be free of self-judgment based on past successes or failures in your personal and professional life.

How others perceive you is important, but not as important as how you perceive yourself. If your fellow Ecademists recognise you as someone who always makes an important contribution, (be it online in the blogs, in the clubs, or offline at events, at meetings), then you will always be in demand.

You may not become an overnight success, but neither will you fail instantly or permanently. Just as your body requires healthy, nourishing food, so does your mind, and remember that although there are many things in your commercial and personal life you cannot control, you can always control your attitude and how you respond to different circumstances.

While your time and how it is spent may be subject to the demands of partners, customers and others, your mind is the one thing that cannot be controlled by anyone but you. Your time is your most important asset & needs to be managed very carefully, so spend it with people who share your desire to succeed on Ecademy. (Not surrounded with negative people.)

I am of the opinion there are two types of people in this world – 'drains' and 'radiators'. Ecademy.com is full of radiators and opportunities. Establish your own philosophy for success, and stick with it, regardless what the rest of the world does.

Many new people just starting in networking hesitate to approach friends or family, or indeed complete strangers. In fact it is estimated that only one in ten are actually comfortable in talking to strangers. This means however, that for the vast majority of people, it is their own misgivings, fears and doubts that are hindering them.

Many of these same people will then hesitate once earning an income out of guilt for accepting money that gives them profit from a friend's purchase. It may be a self-esteem issue - fear of loss of their friends, of facing rejection, of being wrong - and the other conversations are simply 'smoke screens' for the real ego-related issues. You must be 100% happy, and confident with the product, service or opportunity you are promoting. If you're not, then you're not going to be able to convince others. Conversely, if you are confident, then by adopting the right mindset, you will be able to enthuse others, and simply relay the facts, features and benefits of what you have to offer, and how you can help others meet their goals and objectives.

Adopt the right mindset

Describe how you feel about the products and services you offer. Be as honest and as enthusiastic as you possibly can.

_____

_____

_____

_____

_____

---

30 Reasons why people connect with each other

- To make money
- To save money
- To generate referrals
- To reduce stress
- To save time
- To be better organised
- To increase enjoyment – of life, or business
- To help others less fortunate
- To make their work easier
- To be cleaner
- To feel opulent
- To be entertained
- To look younger

- To become more efficient
- To avoid or save effort
- To escape or avoid pain
- To access opportunities
- To feel safe
- To conserve energy
- To become more fit and healthy
- To attract the opposite sex
- To protect their family
- To protect their reputation
- To feel superior
- To communicate better
- To preserve the environment

What Needs of others, can you meet/help?

_____

_____

_____

_____

_____

_____

What Benefits can/do you offer other people?

_____

_____

_____

_____

_____

_____

Opportunities are Everywhere on Ecademy.com

One of the first things you need to establish very quickly, is what exactly do you want to achieve, and who is a likely candidate to help you achieve your goals and objectives.

As you will discover in Part Two of the book, you will stumble across opportunities in many different areas on the website.

- People's Profiles
- The Blogs on the Front Page
- The Club forums
- Marketplace ads
- Meetings, workshops and regional events
- Newsletters, personal messages and emails

Decide on what your aims and objectives are, for example:

- To find out what the market place wants
- To test different marketing approaches
- To generate new ideas
- To meet new contacts
- To develop and learn new skills
- To find a new job/employment/career
- To find new suppliers
- To create a new sales channel/generate more sales
- To pursue your hobbies, interests or past times
- To generate more referrals and JV opportunities

What resources/solutions do you really need NOW?

_____

_____

_____

_____

_____

Before you proceed, ask yourself five very important questions:-

1. Who do you want to reach (what is your criteria)?

_____

2. How are you going to reach them?

_____

3. Why do you want to reach them?

_____

4. What can you do for them?

_____

5. What can they do for you?

_____

The biggest single mistake everybody makes when new to networking, and how to avoid it ...

Stop Wasting Time!

The most common mistake made by the average person in networking is that they waste time trying to sell, manipulate, pester, and persuade prospects to buy. A lot of time and energy is devoted to activities that will inevitably lead to ... nothing. You will generate more sales, referrals, mutual opportunities and expand your network with less effort, when:

- You learn to focus your efforts on helping others

- You stop thinking of prospective customers as prey, for you are not a big game hunter

- You treat your prospects with respect, and are respected by them in return.

- You offer something for FREE that is of value to your intended prospect

- You start by making a list of potential targets, suspects or prospects

> You MUST focus on your contacts needs and wants.
>
> Be sympathetic to the other person's ideas and desires.

Create a Story

To help build your network of contacts and present your offering to your network of contacts, you need to create a personal story that succinctly explains the benefits of what you have to offer and share with others.

This is important because it is exclusively yours and is the foundation for your belief and commitment to your product or service.

Your 'story' should include what moved you to action and what propelled you to use or offer the product or service you're selling, or why customers and clients like it, and what benefits they've found and how you can help others that you introduce into your network.

Remember, at the end of the day people buy people – many people involved in networking forget this, and selfishly think about themselves, as opposed to how they can help others.

The people who expand their networks the fastest, are those who offer elements of their skills, experience, knowledge, advice, contacts, ideas, help or support for FREE.

The giving networker who expects nothing in return will leave a long lasting positive impression on the receiving party, thus increasing the likelihood of them recommending you or referring you to someone in their network of friends, colleagues or contacts. This will inevitably mean that you may receive a reciprocal benefit directly, or indirectly in due course.

To help you prepare your story, you'll need some powerful sound bites, for example:

- When was your business formed?
- The problem your product/service can fix/solve
- Who are the founders/owners of the business?
- The needs your products/service can address
- Has the company won any awards?
- What motivates you and makes you tick
- What are the products/services you're selling?
- What values you stand for, and interests you have
- Have the products/services won any awards?
- What achievements you've had in your business life
- Have the products/services had any good publicity?
- What achievements you've had in your personal life
- What are the facts, features, benefits of what you offer?
- Do you have any testimonials from satisfied clients?
- What level of help and support do you offer?
- How are you different from your competitors?
- Think in terms of your prospect's needs and wants.
- Do you offer a money back guarantee or a guaranteed level of service?

Think about these various points when crafting your profile on Ecademy.com. Think about how you can help others in the network, and – how they might be able to help you too. Write your personal story

Write a personal story about the products, services and the company you work for, and WHY you think its brilliant..

Networking Principle #2

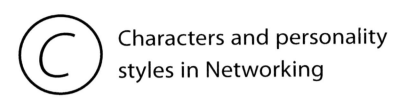

Characters and personality styles in Networking

You may have heard that "People buy People", more importantly, People buy from people they like.

Let's take this, a little step further in helping you understand how to interact and relate to the four different styles of networker you will come across, and the four different styles of Personality that all people belong too.

First of all, let's look at the four different types of networker:-

- The Loner
- The Socialiser
- The User
- The Power Networker

The Loner
The Loner tends to do the majority of things by themselves. They tend to work alone, or in isolation and can sometimes come across as being aloof or superior. This type of networker tends to ask for help as a last resort or upon impending deadlines.

The Socialiser
The Socialiser tends to befriend everyone, appears very popular, but not systematic, doesn't follow up, and will need chasing. Quite often, they don't listen to the needs of their prospects and contacts, and they will move on to the next relationship quickly.

The User

The user will have a large rolodex, or personal organiser, and can sometimes be perceived a "hunter" at the first meeting or encounter. They tend to keep score of introductions and favours offered, and tend to transmit rather than receive information. Their focus tends to be on what's in it for them, rather than what they can do for those in their network.

The Power Networker

The Power Networker tends to have a positive, friendly and sharing disposition, and be happy and willing to share information, resources and contacts, and not afraid to ask for help if they need it. They also tend to proactively network online and offline using a well organised and structured system.

DISC Personality Profiling

ACTIVE People-Oriented	ACTIVE Task-Oriented
Influencing/Inspiring	Dominant/Driver
Stable/Steady	Compliant/Correct
PASSIVE People-Oriented	PASSIVE Task-Oriented

Another way of categorising the different types of individuals you will meet when networking is by using the DISC system.

In the early 1920's, an American psychologist named William Moulton Marston developed a theory to explain people's emotional responses. Until that time, work of this kind had been mainly confined to the mentally ill or criminally insane, and Marston wanted to extend these ideas to cover the behaviour of ordinary individuals. In order to test his theories, Marston needed some way of measuring the behavioural styles he was trying to describe. His solution was to develop his own technique to measure four important factors.

The factors he chose were:

- Dominance
- Influence
- Steadiness
- Compliance

You will be able to determine which of the four personality styles relates to your networking contacts by combining the interpretations of each of the four styles in the following pages.

Combine this with identifying which type of networker they are and the communication medium they prefer, and you have a very powerful system for gaining rapport and communicating with your fellow networkers.

In 1926, Marston published his findings in a book entitled The Emotions of Normal People, which included a brief description of the system he had developed. From these humble beginnings, the DISC system has grown to become probably the most widely used assessment tool in the world.

Read our overview of each of the personality types in the following pages, to identify which trait best describes you, and use it to help you communicate, and provide information to your prospects.

Combining the DISC insights with the different types of networker, you will be able to start growing your network, communicate more effectively, and create more opportunities.

Use the DISC profiling system to inspire, energise, and empower you for your very own networking transformational experience, but more importantly put it into practice when communicating with family, friends or work colleagues before you start practicing with your networking prospects.

Dominance 'D'

The High-D profile is often described as the 'Autocrat', and for good reason. Dominance is the factor of control and assertiveness, and with no other high factors in the profile to balance this, the pure High-D can be remarkably domineering, and even overbearing at times.

This type of person has a very high need to achieve, and because of this they are often ambitious and competitive, striving aggressively to achieve their goals. They are dynamic and adaptable, and show a decisiveness and capacity for direct leadership.

Keywords and phrases to describe a 'D' networker

- Adventuresome – Trying something new
- Decisive – Making quick decisions
- Assertive – Causing action
- Direct – Taking charge
- Inventive – Solving problems
- Original – Creative Thinker
- Self-reliant – Accepting Challenges
- Self-starter – Motivated to begin
- Fast-paced – Getting to the point
- Individualistic – Completing tasks
- Competitive – Wanting to "win"
- Self-assured – Confident about abilities

If your networking prospect is a 'D', they will want and need

- Authority
- Directness
- Variety
- Adventure
- Individual accomplishments
- Freedom

Others may perceive a 'D' type person as

- Intimidating
- Insensitive to others
- Impatient with others

D's perform and 'respond' best, when they are ...

- Left to get the problem solved quickly
- Given brief, direct answers
- Provided with a variety of projects
- Provided with challenging work
- Provided with options
- Congratulated on their achievements
- Don't question their every action

Who do you know, who has a **Dominant** personality style?

_____   _____

_____   _____

_____   _____

Influence 'I'

Influence is the factor of communication. It is for this reason that profiles of this kind are often referred to as 'Communicator' profiles - they describe confident, outgoing and gregarious individuals who value contact with other people and the development of positive relations.

Keywords and phrases to describe an 'I' type networker:

- Warm – Relating to people
- Charming – Desiring to help others

- Positive – Looking on the positive side
- Persuasive – Making a favorable impression
- Playful – Having a sense of humor
- Talkative – Express thoughts & feelings
- Sympathetic – Listening to others
- Extrovert – outgoing personality
- Emotional – sensitive and feeling deeply
- Professional – Concerned about appearance
- People-oriented – like to work with people
- Eager to please – Looking for recognition

If your prospect is an 'I', they want and need:

- To help others
- To interact
- To be noticed, included
- Recognition
- Freedom of expression
- Freedom from control

Others may perceive an 'I' type person as:

- Not detailed enough in their direction
- Superficial in their approach
- Lack of follow through

'I's perform and respond best, when they are:

- Allowed to converse frequently
- Allowed to verbalize their ideas

- Acknowledged for their ideas
- Listened to and asked for their suggestions
- Allowed flexibility

Who do you know, who has an **Influential** personality style?

_____   _____

_____   _____

_____   _____

Steadiness 'S'

Steadiness is the factor of patience, calmness and gentle openness, and a pure High-S personality will reflect these qualities. They are generally amiable and warm-hearted, being sympathetic to others' points of view, and valuing positive inter-action with others. They are not outgoing by nature, however, and rely on other, more assertive, people to take the lead.

Keywords and phrases to describe an 'S' type networker

- Relaxed – Work at an even, relaxed pace
- Even-tempered – Not overly emotional
- Controlled – Cooperating with others
- Reserved – Not speaking up, loyal, stable
- Concerned – security conscious
- Modest – no bragging of accomplishments
- Predictable – Follow procedures/patient
- Low-keyed – Concentrating on the task

If your prospect is an 'S', they want and need:

- Identification with a group
- Appreciation
- Time to plan, adjust
- Stability and traditional procedures
- Credit for work

Others may perceive an 'S' type person as:

- Indecisive
- Indirect in their directions
- Hesitant to implement needed change

'S's perform best, when they are:

- Placed in a team setting
- Given sincere appreciation
- Given a comfortable structure

Who do you know, who has a **Steadiness** personality style?

_____   _____

_____   _____

_____   _____

Compliance 'C'

Passive by nature, often reticent and aloof, people with this kind of personality can give an impression of coldness or disinterest. Highly Compliant personalities are often surprisingly ambitious and have lofty goals, but their innate lack of assertiveness and unwillingness to become involved in confrontational situations makes it difficult for them to achieve these goals directly.

Keywords and phrases to describe a 'C' person are:

- Accurate – Emphasizing facts and data
- Curious - Analyzing
- Task-oriented – Follow directions
- Consistent – Working with control
- Diplomatic – Avoiding conflict
- Logical – Concentrating on detail
- Precise – Checking for accuracy
- Cautious – Worrying about mistakes
- Restrained – Controlling emotions
- Orderly – Organizing work area
- Conscientious – Making lists
- Critical – Criticizing performance

If your prospect is a 'C', they want and need:

- Facts and Data
- Order and rules
- Predictable environment
- Evidence
- Reassurance
- No sudden changes

Others may perceive a 'C' type person or networker as:

- Overly perfectionistic
- Aloof
- Hampering creativity in others with their desire to stick to the rules

'C's perform, and "respond" best, when they are:

- Ideas are supported with accuracy

- Not criticized directly
- Working in an established environment
- Given a step-by-step approach
- Told of changes before they occur
- Given proof and evidence to prove ideas

Who do you know, who has a **Compliant** personality style?

_____   _____

_____   _____

_____   _____

The Networking Funnel ™

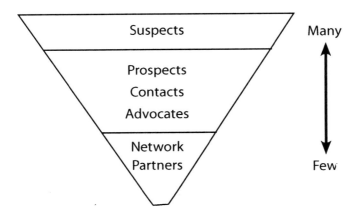

Suspects are at the start of your networking funnel, these are the people that appear to be open to being approached, and have a profile on Ecademy with their full contact details added.

Prospects are the people who meet your criteria and can help you reach your personal and commercial objectives.

Contacts are prospects who you have asked for advice or support, or offered your own assistance in return.

Advocates are openly promoting (advocating) you and your services to others in the network, and you are reciprocating.

Partners are the people you are having the most frequent contact with, and have a much higher level of mutual trust.

Building Relationships using your Networking Funnel ™

(Questions to use)

- What's the biggest project you're working on right now?
- How can I help you?
- Can you tell me a bit more about what you do?
- Who do you know who might be able to help me with … ?
- Who do you know who might be interested in … ?
- If you were me, what would you do?
- Who on Ecademy, would you recommend I speak to?
- Where on Ecademy, would I find … ?
- How would you like to proceed in taking the next step?
- How can we make this happen?
- How can we turn this into a win/win?
- What do you recommend/advise?
- Who would you recommend to … ?
- Who do you know that is an expert in this field?
- Who do you know that is well connected?
- What have you found to work well for you?

The above questions are simply guidelines to help you probe, enquire, and seek out the best ways to make progress towards

your goals and objectives with the help and assistance from people at different stages in your Networking Funnel™.

Feel free to personalise, customise and use the questions by phone, by email, by SKYPE, by MSN messenger or in person.

Networking principle #3

 Arouse interest in others with a great Elevator pitch

Elevator Pitch

With the aid of your "personal story", you can create a more brief impacting, and memorable description of what you do. You can then use your Elevator Pitch, to help answer the "What do you do?" question, that most networking prospects will ask you.

- Be wary of being too complete and being too vague
- Have a simple concept of how using your product or service can benefit the client, that is easy to understand and relate to
- Ensure you pass the "so what" test

There is a very simple formula:

- Create Your Elevator pitch
- Practice different ways of using your elevator pitch
- Timing is everything
- Ask for another 10 seconds.
- Get their feedback

Create Your Elevator pitch, for example:

I run my own life coach business, helping individuals and businesses identify and achieve their goals, so that they become more productive, profitable, and satisfied. Is there anything you would like to be, do or have?

or

We offer a carpet and upholstery cleaning service, 24 hours a day, seven days a week, complete with money back guarantee? Do you require any upholstery or carpets cleaned?

or

I run my own marketing consultancy helping small businesses to generate more traffic, value and revenue to their website or their money back. Would you like more traffic and revenue via your website?

or

I run my own business, helping individuals improve their physical, mental and financial circumstances, so that they live a more fulfilling, less stressful and rewarding life. Is there anything you would like to be, do or have?

Select an elevator pitch from the examples above, personalise it, change the wording in it until you are happy it accurately describes you, and what you offer.

Practice it daily, and use it daily.

Use this in conjunction with your own personal story. By adding a question at the end of your elevator pitch, you will force the prospect to continue speaking with you, instead of saying "so what".

Thus, you are now able to qualify and generate an interest in what you do with 100% of the people you talk to, write to or meet.

Take note, and pay attention how people react when you explain who you are and what you do.

By asking a question at the end of your elevator pitch, you have told them what you do, and if they answer, you've qualified them, and are now determining exactly what it is their goals/ objectives are, so you can tell them about your product or service, and how you can help them.

Let them identify quickly how you can help them.

Write down your elevator pitch of 50 words or less:

_____

_____

_____

_____

_____

_____

Write down your elevator pitch of 30 words or less:

_____

_____

_____

_____

_____

Write down your elevator pitch of 12 words or less:

_____

_____

_____

Different ways of using your elevator pitch

Use your elevator pitch on:

- the telephone, when phoning others
- your telephone answer machine or on your voice mail
- when leaving a message on some one else's voice mail
- when people respond to your adverts
- on a talking email
- in your sales letters/covering letters
- on your business card
- when you introduce yourself to someone in person.

Timing is everything

If you are on the phone, when introducing yourself, and BEFORE you launch into your elevator pitch, ensure you ask the 5 magic words:

"Do you have a moment?".

You must find out if the prospect is free and able to speak to you at the time/point when you call. If they say NO, simply say "OK, I'll call back later" and END the call.

DO NOT PROCEED ANY FURTHER.

If you do continue going straight into your pitch, your prospect will get angry as its not convenient, and will terminate the call.

If they do say they have a moment, then go straight into your elevator pitch. Otherwise, DO NOT PROCEED.

Call back at a more convenient time.

Ask for another 10 seconds.

Once your prospect says that they are FREE to speak, then ask: "I was calling to see if I could tell you a little about my new business, and perhaps identify how we might be of benefit to each other?"

or

"I was calling to see if I could take a few moments to enquire if you would like to save money on all your stationery purchases, and if perhaps, you can help me?"

By doing this, you are NOT asking them to buy something, or to make an appointment with you, it also means that by asking if you can tell them about what you do, that they can't respond by saying very negative statements to you, and if they do say NO, at least you found out very quickly that they are not interested, and you can go on to your next prospect.

> *Fine tune your elevator pitch with your networking prospect in mind, and how you can help them. You may also want to tweak it, by explaining what you do, and the skills or expertise you offer. Remember, your reason for networking with others is to find out how you can help each other.*

Using Your Elevator Pitch

on the phone
(can be tweaked for both selling & networking)

1. Find the decision maker
Can you tell me who deals with _____?
Can I have their email address/direct line number please?

2. Ask if they are free to speak
Do you have a moment/minute?

3. Introduce yourself
" Hi my name is _____ and we specialise in _____ helping businesses to
_____

I was wondering, if we might be of benefit to each other, and explore the possibility of a collaboration in some shape, manner or form."

Or

Mr X, I'm _____ with _____. We specialise in (fill in with the ultimate result prospects want and get from you, i.e., "helping organisations improve the efficiency of their company by _____"). Depending on what you're doing now, and your objectives, this might be something worth taking a look at. (Now you ask permission to continue the call) "I'd like to ask a few questions to see if you'd like more information."

4. Hit them with your ONE or TWO benefit statement

What if … you could _____
Would that be of interest to you?

What if ... you could _____
Would that be of interest to you?

5. If they start asking questions, simply say:

"Do you have a pen, Why not take a peek at my profile on Ecademy, or on our website at www. ...".

Or

"I'm in your area next week, when would be a good time to meet up for a chat, so we can explore how we might be of help to each other. When's good for you? Tues or Wed?"

6. If they don't, then simply move in for the close

"Do you have a pen, Why not take a peek at my profile on Ecademy, or on our website at www. ...".

Or

I'm in your area next week, when would be a good time to meet up for a chat, so we can explore how we might be of help to each other. When's good for you? Tues or Wed?

7. Don't forget to add your appointments to your meeting schedule on Ecademy.com

How to Double Your Appointment & Referral Rate

Can you remember your first business card? Were you proud of the moment you first showed it to someone else? Can you remember their response? Can you remember their initial reaction to all the hard work and effort you had gone to, to create the ideal corporate image for your business?

Unfortunately throughout your business life, the majority of people who you give your business cards to, are not and will not be as enthusiastic about your business card as you.

A simple way to generate more appointments and referrals is to distribute more cards to more people, every single day.

I have a simple formula for business card marketing:-

$$\frac{N + D}{I + R} = B$$

Network and **Distribute** your cards.

But above all ...

Incentivise people to **retain** your card, to create new **Business.**

Essential Business Card Questions

- Do you have a business card?
- What information have you got printed on your cards?
- Is the information/numbers/email address up-to-date?
- How many did you get printed, and when?
- How many have you distributed in the last 4 weeks?
- Who did you give them to, and have you followed up?
- Is your elevator pitch printed on the back of your card?
- Is anything printed on the back of your card?
- Where do you store/keep your cards?
- Have you a CD rom based business card?
- Where and how often do you distribute your cards?
- Does you card give people a reason to call you?
- Can people instantly recognise what it is you "do"?
- Do you keep your business cards in your car glove box?
- What do you say when you give someone your card?
- For every X cards you hand out, how much do you earn?
- How often do you follow up people you've given a card to?
- What do you do when someone hands you their card?
- Do you offer a compliment when receiving a business card?

For a FREE seminar on business card marketing, go to:
www.leadgenerationmba.com/Business_card_marketing.htm

What I have learnt so far:

Networking principle #4

 Dos and Don'ts of Networking

Networking Dos:-

- Be proactive and positive, and do show up for meetings
- Be visible, and well liked, offer to help others
- Learn about your prospects before contacting them (Their Website, "Google them", or their Ecademy profile)
- Be friendly, warm and sincere
- Be enthusiastic, and plan your networking activities well
- Have your elevator pitch and personal story prepared
- Try and remember people's names and faces
- Be persistent and tenacious
- Contribute and add value where possible in blogs, meetings, clubs etc
- Carry your business cards with you at all times
- Write a TO DO list everyday of the things you have to do
- Sit next to strangers at events to help grow your network
- Follow up, follow up, follow up

Networking Don'ts:-

- Don't lose sight of your goals and objectives
- Don't make it difficult for people to contact you
- Don't get lazy

- Don't expect too much from others
- Don't forget to regularly update your business cards
- Don't ask for a sale straight away
- Don't forget networking is a two way street
- Don't be too impatient
- Don't let your efforts stagnate
- Don't be too pushy – let them find you
- Don't contact people only when you need something
- Don't be insensitive to other's beliefs, values or culture
- Don't go for quantity instead of quality in your network
- Don't expect to get something for nothing
- Don't spread yourself too thinly
- Don't forget to regularly update your Ecademy Profile
- Don't say YES too often
- Don't let your marketing costs get out of hand
- Don't lose your momentum
- Don't make unjustifiable claims or statements
- Don't rely on anyone else – depend on yourself
- Don't make promises you can't keep
- Don't expect your network contacts to give referrals
- Don't rush people into business relationships
- Don't forget to follow up, follow up, follow up

Networking principle #5

(E) Engage, Enthuse & Encourage
      those in your network

One of the easiest ways to engage or connect with people is to simply contact them by email, introduce yourself, and ask how you can help them. You could also place an ad on Ecademy's Marketplace and follow them up by phone, email, personal message or SKYPE (www.skype.com).

"Hi Stuart, Fraser Hay here.

I thought I'd drop you a line, just to say "HI" and to find out if we may be of help/benefit to each other. I'm based up here in Scotland, 60 miles North West of Aberdeen and 4 miles past the back of beyond.

For a little more about me click here.

For a few comments from other ecademists, click here.

What sort of projects are you working on at the moment?

If any of them require a marketing, or online marketing input, I'd be happy to help out … if I can. If there's anything you find of interest/value in my profile, or if you'd like to just touch base and have a chat or swap a few ideas, by all means please get in touch.

My direct line is 01542 840101, or feel free to IM or email me."

You can enthuse and encourage people to join your network by offering helpful hints, tips, and advice that can assist them in the development of their network or business. Feel free to personalise this email and send it to up to 100 new subscribers each day. (Refer to page 97 for more info contacting new subscribers.)

Hi Dan, Fraser Hay here.

This is not just a wee note to welcome you to ecademy.

I WANT TO SHARE SOMETHING WITH YOU THAT'S REALLY USEFUL …

1. Your Fifty Words in your profile, and the first line of your profile text are spidered by google, so try and use keywords associated with your website to help get you found FAST.

2. Use the first line of your profile to contain KEYWORD phrases, that are hyperlinked back to your main website. This can boost your Link Popularity, Page Rank and bring traffic.

3. Please feel free to check out my profile and LISTEN to my wee message, to see if I can help you in any way and if I can, please don't hesitate to contact me.

4. Also, why not explore placing an ad on Marketplace here on ecademy to help generate some leads and enquiries for your products and services. I've written a wee blog on how to get the best from Marketplace. Remember, The Headline, and TAGS (Keywords) that you use in your market-place ads are also spidered by Google.com to help give your ads wider distribution, for some more tips

in maximising your response from Marketplace, then click here

5. Visit www.leadgenerationmba.com for a FREE online seminar with some ideas on how to generate leads, prospects, enquiries and sales your products and services.

Feel free to call me on 01542 840101, or Message me via my ecademy profile, even if its just to bounce an idea off me, or to pick my brains.. Once again, welcome onboard and if I can help you in anyway, just let me know.

Regards,

One of the easiest ways to enlist the help of others is to simply ask for their help personally, or you could post a question in a blog or club forum, (more about that in part 2).

Hi Eric, Fraser Hay here.

I wonder if you can help me? I am currently in the marketplace for a print quote for some new leaflets and am also looking for some advice. Is this something you can assist me with, or do you know anyone who can?

Can I suggest we arrange a mutually convenient time to hook up either by Phone, Skype or MSN Messenger to have a chat and discuss mutual opportunities and how we might be able to be of benefit to each other.

My direct line is 01542 840101, or feel free to IM or email me via my profile..

I look forward to hearing from you.

Regards

If you operate in the Business-to-Business arena, you may find this document useful to help give you ideas of different industries, or sectors to target. You could then search for those industries in a particular town, city, county or region via google. com, yell.com, yellow pages or Ecademy.com

http://www.leadgenerationmba.com/industries.pdf

You may also wish to place a blog, or advert in Marketplace on Ecademy.com, or start your own club. (More in part 2).

Communicating with your fellow Ecademists

Once you've contacted your prospective addition to your network using some of the methods outlined previously, or if a prospect responds to your advert, email, letter or phone call, you then need to decide HOW you are going to give them the information about you, your business, products or services and how you can help them. Your ability to create rapport with prospects, and communicate with them on a "level" that is "comfortable" for them is vital at this stage in the networking process.

The hardest part of any business is to generate leads and enquiries, but you'd be amazed by the number of people who fail to follow up a prospect simply because they said "NO" the first time they were asked or simply just failed to be proactive, or get in touch each time someone visited their Ecademy profile or read one of their ads on Ecademy Marketplace.

If someone visits your profile on Ecademy.com, joins your club, or reads one of your ads on Ecademy's marketplace, you will be notified by email with the member's details.

This is very powerful, and a helpful reminder to follow-up.

Your ability to follow up and connect with people and encouraging them to join your network is pivotal to your success in ANY business, and as a professional networker we have a fantastically simple process to help you do this.

Our unique process maximises the best possible conversions for you.

In my experience, there are four types of people who will respond to your proactive networking efforts:

- **Serious enquiries**
- **Interested parties**
- **Time wasters and 'experts'**
- **Pitchers** of other opportunities.

We have a method of dealing with each of these types of individual, to ensure you get maximum conversion, and maximum revenues.

Serious enquiries

These guys are hot to trot, and will respond positively, giving you the necessary information and will be keen to learn more, often asking questions, and wanting to progress the relationship immediately.

Get their business card or personal details and email address immediately, identify their needs and interests, explain how you can help them, and offer them something of value for nothing, to further progress the relationship

With serious enquiries, you want to be seen to be professional and organised. So we give them the information they want.

Interested Parties

These guys dither, and will come up with excuses why they cant or wont progress matters with you at the moment etc

Interested parties tend to be the people who appear frequently on your profile hits, having visited your Ecademy profile a number of times, and also your Marketplace hits, having viewed your ads a number of times too.

This is fair enough, everyone's timing is different, they probably want to say YES, but not just today, If they gave you their details, then use the follow up advice we offer in part 2.

Quite often it will take 4 or 5 follow ups (or more) to get your desired result. Chances are the prospect does want your product or service, or create a mutually beneficial relationship with you and quite often they just need time to relax, reflect and make an informed decision.

These are the guys who will probably ask lots of questions – THIS IS GOOD – and we'll deal with this later too. Again, the object of dealing with these types of prospect, is simply to establish how they would like the information, and give it to them via their preferred mode of communication, which we'll cover in a minute.

Time Wasters and 'Experts'
Hard to establish at this stage, but we still want to be seen to be professional and organised.

Quite often they're just information gathering and "sussing you out". So we give them the information they want, or direct them to your profile or website.

Pitchers of other opportunities, products and services.
You will sometimes get people responding to your networking efforts, pitching you straight away on other opportunities, or trying to sell you their products and services. This is to be expected, as everyone's way of doing things is different. Simply offer to enter into dialogue to identify areas of mutual benefit and offer them to review all your information, and to send you,

theirs. Again, the object of dealing with these types of prospects, is simply to establish how they would like the information, and give it to them.

How to communicate with Ecademists

Not only will you get different types of respondents to your promotional efforts, they will also have a preferred way to communicate with you too, in one of three ways -

> Visual: (by reading, or looking at something or someone)

> Auditory: by listening/talking)

> Kinesthetic: feelings/human interaction/touch)

Even though you plan your time, and proactively research and contact people to join your network, quite often people involved in networking 'lose' up to 66% of their prospects, simply because they didn't communicate effectively with their prospect on the first point of contact.

If you offer to SEND the information to a prospect, but they actually prefer to HEAR the information, you will lose them.

If you start doing your sales presentation over the phone, and they prefer to STUDY and read the information instead, you will lose them.

If you offer to SEND the information to a prospect, but they actually prefer to MEET you in PERSON, you will lose them.

Quite often, in your very first conversation with your prospect, you will be able to determine what their preferred method of communication is.

Type of Prospect: Visual or 'V'

Description: If they are a 'V' person, they typically stand, or sit, with their heads and/or body erect with their eyes up, and will be breathing from the top of their lungs. They often sit forward in the chair or on the edge of the chair.

They tend to be more organised, neat, sharp dressers and orderly. More deliberate. Visual people, tend to be more appearance oriented, and funnily enough, sometimes quieter.

They tend to be good spellers. They Memorise by visualising information, and can often have an eye for detail.

However, they often have trouble remembering verbal instructions, and can quickly get bored by your long verbal explanations because their minds tend to wander.

Signals: They might respond by email, personal message, SKYPE or visit a url in an ad. As they would rather read than be read to. Or if they are responding by phone, they might say "looks good to me", or "Lets see what it is you do", or "I see", "Can I see more information", "I'd like a look at your information/opportunity/profile", "Send me the details." Etc.

Action: If so, then you should offer to SEND THEM the information by a personal message, email or invite them to take a look at your profile or website, so they can READ your information, and ask them to contact you with any questions or if they need help or require further assistance.

If you are following up a 'V' person, always follow up in writing (ideally by email) tell them you are happy to answer any questions in writing to put their mind at rest.

Type of Prospect: Auditory or 'A'

Description: If they are an 'A' person, they typically talk to themselves, and are easily distracted by noise. They often move their lips when they read words. They can assimilate information quickly and repeat things back to you easily.

They may find the financial aspects and writing more difficult and spoken language easier. They like music and learn by listening.

They memorise by steps, procedures, and sequence. An auditory person is often interested in being told how they're doing, and responds to a certain set of words or tone of voice.

Signals: The majority of auditory people respond to adverts with telephone numbers in. They want to hear the facts quickly. They might say "Sounds good to me", "Can you tell me more about it", or "I'd like to speak with...", "I'm listening", "Good to talk to you" etc etc.

Action: If so, then you want to invite them to "listen" to a short presentation/recording on your website or 0870 telephone number, invite them into a SKYPE call or three-way call or offer to tell them about what you do/offer so they can listen to your information. Invite them to listen to the facts, get their questions answered etc.

If you are following up a 'A' person, follow up by phone or in writing (by email or mail) asking for a convenient time to TELEPHONE THEM or to join you in a conference call or three-way call so you can answer any questions they might have.

Type of Prospect: Kinesthetic or 'K'
Description: If they are a 'K' person, they will typically be breathing from the bottom of their lungs, so you'll see their stomach go in and out as they breathe. Their posture is often more slumped over, and they often move and talk verrrry slooowly, or gently.

They will typically access their feelings and emotions to 'get a feel' for what they're doing. They respond to physical rewards, and touching. They also stand close to people and touch them.

Signals: They are often physically oriented people (athletes). They may move a lot and they memorize by doing, or walking through something. They use words like: "Feelings" "Get in touch", "Hold, "Grasp", "Handle", e.g. "Can I get a handle on what it is you offer", "I've got a good feeling about this", "I'm getting excited", "Can you walk me through what it is I have to do" etc

Action: If so, then you want to invite them to "walk through your sales/information process" so they can "get a handle" of what it is you're offering. You could say "I've got a feeling you're going to like this" or "I got excited when I first found out about it". I'm sure you get the idea…

Invite them to receive a personal presentation from you, so they can experience first hand, what it's all about, and so they can try some of the features and benefits that you'll share with them.

If you are following up a 'K' person, follow up by phone or in writing (by email or mail) asking for a convenient time to TELEPHONE THEM or SKYPE them to join you in a conference call or three-way call so you, or one of your colleagues, can 'personally' answer any questions they might have.

In conclusion, whether it's face-to-face or via the Ecademy website, in that first point of contact, you should be able to determine whether they are a 'V', 'A' or 'K' person, and offer them the appropriate information medium that will appeal to them. You should also focus in on this, when following up prospects, and if you want better conversions on your website then add audio presentations to each of your sales pages

Facts, features, and benefits

Many objections come in the form of questions, of which 80% can easily be overcome by preparing a list of Features and benefits.

In the space below why not write down a list of 10 facts, features and benefits about your products and services.

e.g. We offer a range of personal success programs which means, not only do we help you to Identify your goals, we also help you to pursue them and monitor your performance to ensure you achieve them and can see definitive progress.

Using the words "which means", turns a fact into a benefit.

Fact 1

Which means

Benefit 1

Fact 2

Which means

Benefit 2

Fact 3

Which means

Benefit 3

Fact 4

Which means

Benefit 4

Fact 5

Which means

Benefit 5

Fact 6

Which means

Benefit 6

Fact 7

Which means

Benefit 7

Fact 8

Which means

Benefit 8

Fact 9

Which means

Benefit 9

Fact 10

Which means

Benefit 10

How to Overcome Objections 97.5% of the time on Ecademy.com

Having created rapport with your networking contact, and explained your facts, features and benefits, be prepared for their objections, questions or issues they may have that you will have to overcome if you are after a sale.. Objections occur because of a doubt that your prospect has. It is therefore essential that the objection is dealt with properly, so that the sale will occur.

To overcome objections, use the Mnemonic DATO

D   Define it

A   Agree with their thinking

T   Tip the balance in your favour

O   Overcome it

Step One: D
Define exactly what is being objected to. To do this, repeat the objection back to the prospect – one way is to use the phrase "So, what you're saying, is..".

Step Two: A
Agree with the customer's thinking, NOT what they are objecting to. For example: "I agree, I also don't like the idea of …"

Step Three: T
Tip the balance in your favour, by recapping how your product or service can provide the solution to their needs …

Step Four: O
Overcome the objection by providing the answer to your prospect's satisfaction, and then getting agreement that what has been said/offered is ok. Finally, check there are no other objections.

Frequently Asked Questions

Make a list of Frequently asked questions with answers about your products or service which could double up as a list of possible objections a prospect could make about your product or service, for example Price, delivery times, availability, support, service etc. You may wish to even consider publishing these frequently asked questions on your Ecademy profile or website.

Ensure you write down an answer which includes a benefit.

Q. _____

A. _____

Q. _____

A. _____

Q. _____

A. _____

Continue onto another sheet if required

Networking principle #6

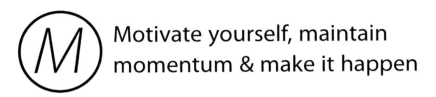

Motivate yourself, maintain momentum & make it happen

Probably one of the most important factors in networking is tenacity and a personal commitment to your business.

The hardest part of any business is to generate leads and enquiries, but you'd be amazed by the number of people who fail to follow up a prospect simply because they said "NO" the first time they were asked. Or that they simply didn't get in touch, despite that their contact details were logged on your profile hits or marketplace ad views pages.

Your ability to follow up prospects and enquiries is pivotal to your success in ANY business, and as a professional networker on Ecademy.com, there are a number of key resources you can use to identify those people who need to be followed up, and we cover them in detail in part 2.

There are a number of different ways, and combinations of different ways that you can communicate with your network.

How do you communicate and follow up your prospects at the moment?

Phone	___	3-Way	___	Teleconf	___
In person	___	Email	___	Combination	___
SKYPE	___	MSN	___	Direct Mail	___

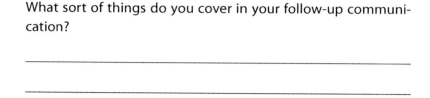

What sort of things do you cover in your follow-up communication?

_____

_____

The objective of following up prospects is to get them to respond and enter into dialogue with you either by phone, email, instant messenger/SKYPE or in person.

Once you are in dialogue with them, and gain rapport, you can overcome any of their objections, (as detailed earlier) put their mind at rest, and ask to progress the relationship.

PLEASE NOTE: It's not uncommon, for it to take four, five or more follow-ups on Ecademy.com, to get the desired result.

Here are some interesting stats and feedback I've received -

- 2% get the desired result on the 1st call / communication
- 3% get the desired result on the 2nd call / communication
- 14% get the desired result on the 3rd call / communication
- 20% get the desired result on the 4th call / communication
- 61% get the desired result, the sale, on their 5th phone call / email / letter or communication

That means you could be losing up to **95%** of your desired networking results, if you don't continually follow-up after your 2nd call or communication.

How do you keep track of all your prospects at the moment?

_____

Ask "why?"

Prospects often say no when they mean not now or because they really do not understand what they have been offered and are declining to act rather than say so. The correct way to respond when a prospect says no is to ask WHY?

This single word is one of your most valuable sales tools and responses. Say your new contact has just declined to purchase your product or service from you, or doesn't want to progress the relationship. You could just accept what he says as final. Remember, he wouldn't have responded, or visited your profile etc if he wasn't interested.

Asking WHY? Helps to further qualify their interest

If a prospect fails to proceed to the next stage in your sales or networking process, you should promptly email or otherwise contact the prospect and ask WHY?

What is the most common reason that people may have turned you down for your product/service or opportunity?

_____

_____

_____

Use the Personal message facility on Ecademy.com to follow up your prospect, then wait 24 hours or so for an answer.

If you still have not heard from the prospect, resend the question with STANDING BY at the top of the message. In other words, make it plain that you want to continue the sales process/dialogue and need further information.

In virtually all cases, when the prospect responds his reason for declining to purchase now will be MONEY (or rather the lack of it.)

That might also mean your price is too high – which means you could lessen the blow by offering your different payment methods and options.

Some people may simply not be able to afford your services, or perhaps be willing to pay the price you ask.

You need to discover just how much money (their budget) the prospect has now, when the prospect will have enough and when he could go ahead. Perhaps the prospect did not know he did not have to pay the whole amount at once. Or perhaps, upon consideration, he finds he has enough for his first payment after all.

Your job is to patiently nudge the prospect to TALK TO YOU, to tell you about his situation, and to give you the information you need to be able to respond appropriately.

I'll be very, very surprised if a prospect actually says they don't like the product or service you have to offer.

Money or budget, (or lack of), is probably the main reason why they decline to buy at any given point.

But it might not be.

Once you know WHY a prospect has declined to buy, it may well be time to brainstorm with a friend, colleague or boss about the prospect and his/her circumstances.

The more you are able to tell your colleague or friend, the more they will be able to help you, and strike the best deal!

Obviously, none of this is possible if you accept NO for an answer from a prospect. Equally, if you are willing to treat an initial no as merely another step in the sales process and to contact the prospect until you get a straight and detailed answer, it may well be possible to get the sale after all.

Note: if the prospect still declines to buy at this time, do not hesitate to sign him up to your club, e-zine or newsletter. This way you can keep marketing to this individual and motivate an eventual sale. I have come across many people who said no initially and then, either immediately or in due course, became good customers.

The key is not letting that "NO" get in the way of your relationship, following up immediately to find out WHY the prospect is saying no now, and both listening carefully to what the prospect says in response and working with the prospect to come up with an ideal solution that's acceptable to both of you.

Quite often networking can be demoralising, and often you need to recharge the mental batteries, and give yourself a motivational kick in the backside, or give yourself an inspirational lift. Why not visit www.pocketmentor.co.uk for more information on our 3-in-1 personal life coach, diary and success system. Check out our free inspirational movies too.

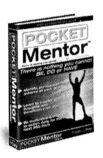

What I have learnt so far:

Networking principle #7

 Your Objectives and Progress revisited

An essential part of networking, is monitoring your progress, against your objectives, and measuring what you have achieved against key mile stones – on a regular basis.

You can measure your success/progress in a number of ways:
- Number of people who have visited your profile/got in touch
- Number of people who are in your network
- Number of people who have joined your club
- Number of people who have read your Marketplace ads
- Number of people who have become prospects/subscribers
- Number of people who have become customers
- Value of sales generated

Some times things don't go according to plan, or people fail to deliver on their promise for whatever reason. So we must ensure our plan stays fluid and can be revisited and adapted often. You'd be surprised how many people don't test new approaches, having found that the last one didn't work.

If you answer NO to any of the questions below, then simply give thought as to how you will tackle it, or alternatively, visit the relevant session in our advanced Lead Generation MBA course at www.leadgenerationmba.com). (Don't forget about your gift voucher on page 134 – very useful). NB the numbers in brackets on the following pages are relating to the relevant session in the Lead Generation MBA Course.

1. Do you update your weekly goals – EVERY WEEK (18)

_____

2. Do you review your TO DO list, and add prospects to your tracking system every day (18)

_____

3. Have you placed an ad, written a blog, added a forum thread in your club, emailed/spoken to a prospect today (11)

_____

4. Do all emails you send contain your details and phone number (02)

_____

5. Do you address all objections promptly & professionally (16)

_____

6. Do you give personal examples to back up what you say (16)

_____

7. Instead of talk/writing about the features, do you talk /write about benefits (16)

_____

8. Do you show testimonials/ask your sales director to back up what you are saying (11)

_____

9. Do you use teleconferencing/seminars to sell educate several prospects at one time? (05)

_____

10. Do you focus on establishing rapport with the prospect? (15)

_____

11. Ensure your emails are not full of technical jargon or buzz words (02)

_____

12. Do you isolate what your prospects are really objecting to and overcome it (16/17)

_____

13. When a prospect says NO, do you ask "Why?" and send a follow up Email/letter (17)

_____

14. Do you give up, as soon as the prospect says "NO" (17)

_____

15. Do you tell the prospect that your product/service is exceptional value (16/17)

_____

16. Do you ensure ALL past and present prospects have been followed up (17)

_____

17. Do you re-visit your master list of warm market prospects regularly by phone/email (13)

_____

18. Do you use the correct communication medium for your "V", "A" & "K" type prospects so they can be presented with the 'correct' information (15)

19. Do you plan your promotional budget weekly, & decide which other methods that you will use to promote your products/services (18)

20. Do you re-visit your "closing" process regularly, and re-evaluate how you interpret Buying signals, Closing techniques and "when to close" etc (16)

21. Are you happy with the number of prospects you generate via personal selling, advertising, direct mail and Ecademy? (18)

22. Do you own, manage, or participate in a direct sales team, affiliate program, or distributor network and want to rapidly increase your sales turnover, income and exposure of your products and services?

Yes? Then visit: www.tdmsolutions.co.uk/intro.php

23. Would you like more newsletter/e-zine signups or more downloads of your e-books or software applications?

Yes? then visit: www.tdmsolutions.co.uk/Ebook_Covers.htm

How to Guarantee Your Future Success

1. Have you got the right mindset?   Yes/No
2. Have you identified the needs you can satisfy?   Yes/No
3. Have you identified the resources/tools you need?   Yes/No
4. Do you know who you want to reach?   Yes/No
5. Have you decided how you'll reach them?   Yes/No
6. Have you decided why you'll reach them?   Yes/No
7. Have you identified what you can do for others?   Yes/No
8. Have you identified what others can do for you?   Yes/No
9. Have you created a personal story?   Yes/No
10. Have you identified that type of networker you are?   Yes/No
11. Have you identified your personality type?   Yes/No
12. Have you crafted your Elevator pitch?   Yes/No
13. Have you listed your facts, features & benefits?   Yes/No
14. What's your preferred mode of communication?   (V, A, K)
15. Have you decided how you'll follow up your prospects? Yes/No
16. Have you decided how you" store prospects details?   Yes/No
17. Have you reviewed/ printed your business cards?   Yes/No
18. Have you identified the reasons why people turn you
     down & got a method for overcoming their objections? Yes/No
19. Have you reviewed your marketing efforts to date?   Yes/No
20. Have you set your goals and objectives?   Yes/No

If you answer No to any of the questions, please refer back to the appropriate section in Part 1 of this book.

What I have learnt so far:

PART TWO

Ecademy – Where Business People Click

Preparing to use Ecademy.com

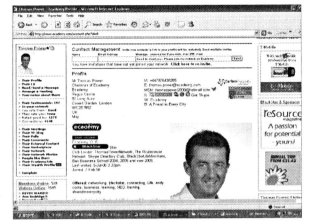

Thomas Power,
Co-Founder and
Chairman of
Ecademy.com

One of the main differences between those who achieve great things in life and those who don't is that successful people learned that they were responsible for their own actions and own successes. No other person can make you successful or keep you from achieving success on Ecademy.com – it is in fact, down to you.

One thing is for sure, if you aspire to succeed on Ecademy.com then you need to demonstrate to others in your network that you can be counted upon. The best rewards and opportunities are waiting for those who can always deliver on their promises.

If you can find a way to do things better, faster or cheaper, you increase your value to everyone you meet on Ecademy, and are guaranteed to be destined for bigger & better things.

As Prime Minister Benjamin Disraeli once said "Action may not always bring happiness, but there is no happiness without action."

The oncoming months will see amazing opportunities for

personal and commercial growth for you. You will develop many personal facets – mentally, emotionally, and if applied correctly – financially.

You can develop these personal facets in three ways:

Through your individual efforts
Helping and connecting with friends, colleagues, partners and prospects by offering advice, guidance, support and knowledge to others. Planning and reaching your personal and corporate goals with the help of the different tools and resources on Ecademy.com

Through your daily use of Ecademy.com
Get yourself into a daily routine, of adding blogs, ads, club forum entries, following up requests for information, profile hits, market place ad respondents. Explore each of the different areas on Ecademy.com, and use them daily.

Through your interaction in your relationships
As a partner, friend, supplier, subscriber, club owner, community member and networker, you will be able to develop a number of new and exciting relationships on a local , regional, national or international basis on Ecademy.

In fact, a new paradigm shift has occurred in the way people network via the introduction of professional networking sites like ecademy.com and thanks to 7 key fundamentals of Thomas Power's (chairman of ecademy.com) mission to have a friend in every city worldwide.

1. The more you do for others, and the more value you add, the more liked you will be

2. The more liked you are the more people know you

3. The more people you know the more contacts you have

4. The more contacts you have the more opportunities you have

5. The more opportunities you have, the wealthier you will be in many ways.

6. The wealthier you feel the more peace of mind you have

7. The more peace of mind the kinder you can be towards others.

The goal of this half of the book is to introduce you to an exciting and rewarding way of doing business and more specifically, to introduce you to the ecademy.com portal and help you raise the profile of you, your products/services, and your business, as you generate lots of new prospects, colleagues, partners, suppliers and customers.

Yours sincerely

Fraser J. Hay

Fraser J. Hay

Click the link for a FREE Seminar on Ecademy Success
http://www.pocketmentor.co.uk/Think_Success.htm

Preparing to Use Ecademy.com

On the next page is a list of several items you may wish to think about at the beginning and end of each day before and after you visit www.ecademy.com.

I have listed some key thought-provoking questions you may wish to review each morning and night in order to maintain the high level of results you will generate with Ecademy.com throughout the year.

You may also wish to combine your daily questions with a "TO DO LIST". An example is located at www.leadgenerationmba.com/TODO.pdf

Get into a good habit of perhaps demonstrating your skills and ability before talking about them to others. Plan your work, and work the plan – every day. Persuading yourself that you can achieve or do something is a strong starting point prior to developing your plan of action, and the longer the delay, the harder it will be to begin.

Please, don't forget that plans seldom work first time. In fact, I have changed my profile over 100 times in recent months, and I've seen me edit the headline in a marketplace ad 4, 5 even 7 times in a day, before I started getting the results I had hoped.

If you have a clear vision of what you want to achieve on Ecademy.com, and a plan that is flexible enough to deal with unexpected obstacles or take advantage of unforeseen opportunities, then start implementing your plan as quickly as possible. Don't forget you can always amend your plan later, but start directing your energies towards your goals.

Daily Thoughts for using Ecademy.com

- What is positive or exciting about my day today?
- What is the one thing I must get done today?
- Who needs my help today?
- How can I help them, add value to what they are doing?
- How can I contribute to my network/Ecademy today?
- What am I willing to do today that'll help my network grow?
- What can I write a blog about today?
- What can I say in my club today?
- Who could I invite into my network today?
- Who could refer new prospects or projects to me today?
- My No.1 goal for today?
- What actions must I take to move me closer to my goal(s)?
- What and how will I advertise my wants and offers on Marketplace today?

Things to ponder as I end each day…

- What 3 good things happened to me today?
- What did I achieve today?
- What can I do tomorrow to increase my network and reach my goals?
- What happened today, that if I could, I would have done differently?
- What can I learn from today?
- How can I ensure I don't make the same mistake again?
- Did I move closer or farther away from my goals for the week? Why?

- Am I ready for tomorrow? Have I planned for tomorrow?
- Have I started my list of things to do for tomorrow

Getting the most from Ecademy.com

Plan Your Time

Spend time planning and organising. Using time to think and plan is time well-spent. Reread your daily questions (on the previous page) every morning & evening.

Set Goals. Goals give you, your life, and the way you spend your time, direction. We cover this in greater detail on the next page.

Prioritise. The 80/20 rule originally stated by the Italian economist Vilfredo Pareto who noted that 80% of the reward comes from 20% of the effort.

Use a TO DO List. Some people thrive using a daily To Do list. Such people may combine a To Do list with their Pocket Mentor for maximum effect.

Be Flexible. Allow time for interruptions and distractions. You have the flexibility to handle interruptions and the unplanned "emergency.".

Consider your biological Prime time. Are you a 'morning person,' a 'night owl' or a late afternoon 'whiz?' Knowing when your best time is and planning to use that time of day for your priorities is effective time management.

Do the right things right. Doing the right thing is effectiveness; doing things right is efficiency. Focus first on effectiveness (identifying what is the right thing to do), then concentrate on efficiency (doing it right).

Practice the art of intelligent neglect. Eliminate from your life trivial tasks or those tasks which do not have long-term consequences for you. Can you delegate or eliminate any of your To Do list? Work on those tasks which you alone can do.

Conquer procrastination. When you are avoiding something, break it into smaller tasks. By doing a little at a time, eventually you'll reach a point where you'll want to finish.

Learn to say "NO." First you must be convinced that you and your priorities are important — that seems to be the hardest part in learning to say "no." Once convinced of their importance, saying "no" to the unimportant in life gets easier.

Reward yourself. Even for small successes, celebrate achievement of goals. Promise yourself a reward for completing each task, or finishing the total job. Then keep your promise to yourself and indulge in your reward.

For a FREE Seminar on Time Management, click on www.pocketmentor.co.uk/Goal_Setting_Time_Management.htm

How to set effective goals
Write down a list of all the things you want to be or become, do or achieve, have or enjoy. Go for it. You can have absolutely everything you desire. Give no thought to cost or material resources.

Write down absolutely everything.

Put your goals in writing, as a commitment to yourself.

Fine tune your list until you are only writing down those things you really desire. Re-write the list frequently and commit to memory, better still – look at it daily.

Expand each item, adding all the details to fully describe the completeness of the goal. (As if you were completing an order form). Beside each goal, set a date for their accomplishment, then write each goal as though it had happened e.g. "By January 01, 2007 I had accumulated £100,000 in new business and 500 new connections in my network."

Pages 87-88 cover an excellent process for you to accurately determine your future goals & objectives based on your previous experiences. You will find this very useful.

For a FREE Seminar on Goal Setting, click the link below:
http://www.pocketmentor.co.uk/Four_step_formula.htm

Don't forget the S.M.A.R.T. rule
Make sure your goals are:

Specific.	Write down exactly what it is you want
Measurable.	How will you know if you have achieved it
Attainable	Make sure you think about HOW you are going to get it
Realistic	Your Goals must be goals that you believe you can achieve
Time bound	Set a target date. It doesn't matter if you miss it, but set one.

Write your action plan, how you are going to achieve your goals.

Break your action plan down into 12 monthly steps. Set your goals for each month, and re-visit your plan at the end of each month. Pocket Mentor from Pocketmentor.co.uk guarantees to help you achieve this.

Remember though, unexpected surprises do happen, so ensure that your plan is adaptable.

Before we can set our goals, we need to fully understand where we are now.

Before we can begin ...

We need to identify our business accomplishments and disappointments for the last 12 months, so that we can learn from them, and plan accordingly for the year ahead with Ecademy.com

1. What have you accomplished in the last 12 months?

_____

2. What have been your disappointments in the last 12 months?

_____

3. How do you explain these disappointments and what have you learned?

_____

4. What will you do differently in the next 12 months?

_____

5. What are your top 10 goals with Ecademy.com?

_____

_____

_____

_____

_____

_____

_____

_____

_____

_____

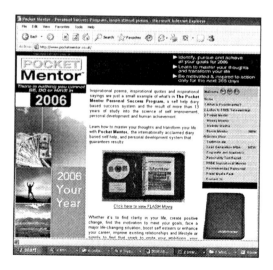

Creating a Profile on Ecademy.com

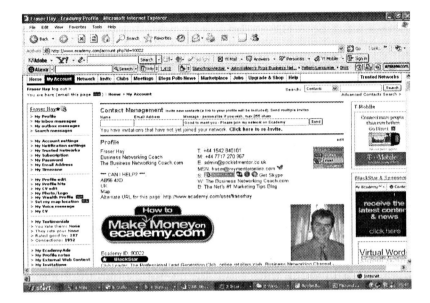

Personal details
Add your full personal details including website address & mobile phone number. Encourage people to contact you by phone, email and SKYPE.com.

Photograph / Logo
Upload a photograph as this will greatly increase hits to your profile. Try and use a recent one, and not one from 20 years ago. Your company or website logo is also a good addition as it helps people to recognise you or your brand.

50 Words
Add the 50 words that best describe you and what you do. Remember these words are searchable across the platform.

Selecting the right keywords here will also help you get found by these same phrases on google.com.

Voice Tag
Consider adding a voice message, as it will help to individualise and personalise your profile and bring it to life.

Graphics / Images
Add more photos, graphics and images to your profile to help liven it up and make it easier to read.

Achievements
Write down any achievements you've had throughout your career, and to help people identify what you're good at, and how you can help them

Websites
We strongly recommend you link to any websites you own, as Ecademy is regularly spidered by google, and can increase your link popularity and Google Page rank.

A good tip is to make the first line of your profile contain keyword loaded links out to your websites.

Benefits. Benefits. Benefits
Give simple compelling reasons why people should contact you, and what you can do for them. Consider offering some-thing for FREE such as a free consultation, free ebook, free chat, free article. Give prospects a good reason to get in touch.

Here are just a few examples of the offerings on my profile.

>FREE Personal Success Seminar
>
>The Four Step Formula for Success
>
>FREE Goal Setting Seminar
>
>How to get whatever you want, when you want it
>
>FREE personal success Seminar

How to Make Money on Ecademy.com with MarketPlace

FREE networking Seminar -

How to Succeed at Business Card Marketing

Skills, Talents and Experience

An important aspect of your profile should be what skills, talent or experience you can offer others. This is important and you need to differentiate yourself from others offering similar products and services. Give examples of what you can do for others, by illustrating how you can help them by linking to case studies, or testimonials.

Signature

Ensure you add your elevator pitch, unique selling point or reason to contact you in your profile signature. This is displayed at the end of each blog or posting you make on the site. Most people tend to add their website address, and elevator pitch here. Here's an example of what I do.

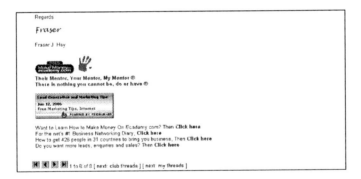

Testimonials

Encourage other people to add testimonials to your profiles. This will help increase your credibility and referrals within the network. To read over 100 of my testimonials, click the link below.

http://www.ecademy.com/module.php?mod=guestbook&id=90022

Who's visited my Profile

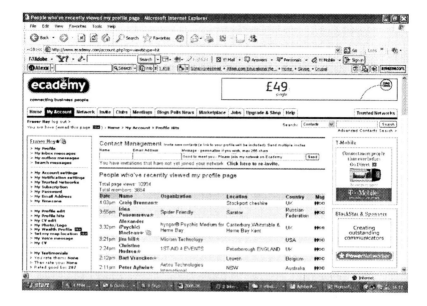

My Profile Hits

By clicking on these links you can see exactly who has viewed your profile recently, and more importantly, you can send them a personal message, simply by clicking on their name. This is an excellent way to start networking, and introducing yourself and following people up who will contact you when you first join. Be prepared for lots of people welcoming you to Ecademy.com and offering you help support, and advice.

For a sample follow up email, please see the next page.

Sample PROFILE follow up email

Hi jeff

Many thanks for taking a peek at my profile …

I'd like to take a closer look at yours, to see if I can identify any common ground or areas of mutual benefit.

In the meantime, should you require any marketing help, advice or guidance, then please feel free to have a listen at any of the audio seminars on my profile, visit my advanced marketing course at www.leadgenerationmba.com, or take a peek at some of the comments from other people here on Ecademy.

May I also suggest that we perhaps hook up by phone or SKYPE later in the week. (My Skype ID is pocketmentor), to see if we can identify some areas of mutual interest, as I'd love to find out a bit more about what you do and how we might be of benefit to each other.

My direct telephone line is on my profile.

Regards

Fraser

My Network

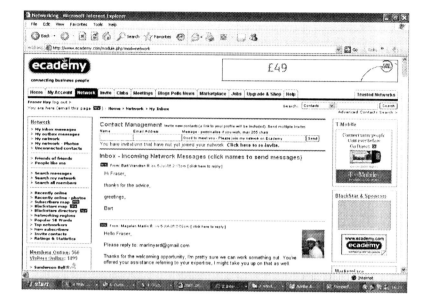

My Inbox Messages/My Outbox Messages

This is an excellent feature allowing you to send emails and messages to people in your network. This can be an excellent way of contacting people you find on the website.

Details of a marketing test I did, are detailed on the next page where I received 83 responses from 140 emails sent, and if you haven't worked that out yet… it was 59% response. Not only do I prove it to you on the next page, I also provide you with a copy of the email I sent.

A 59% response to an Email Campaign

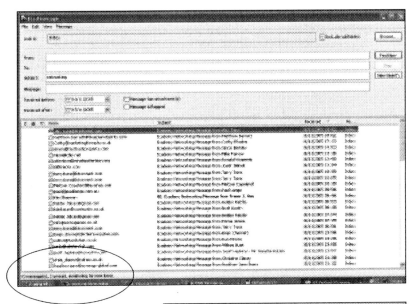

*My Inbox after
140 Messages sent*

83 / 140 = 59% Response

Sample Prospecting Email

Please note, this email is a simple, polite, and professional email introducing myself, and asking the recipient to get in touch. Nothing more. Nothing less.

> Hi William,
>
> Fraser Hay here.
>
> As you're a Blackstar member, I thought I'd drop you a line, just to say "HI", and to find out if we may be of help/benefit to each other.
>
> I'm based up here in Scotland, 60 miles North West of Aberdeen and 4 miles past the back of beyond.
>
> For a little more about me click <u>here</u>.
>
> For a few comments from other ecademists, click <u>here</u>.
>
> What sort of projects are you working on at the moment?
>
> If any of them require a marketing, or online marketing input, I'd be happy to help out if I can.
>
> If there's anything you find of interest/value in my profile, or if you'd like to just touch base and have a chat or swap a few ideas, by all means please get in touch.
>
> My direct line is 01542 840101, or feel free to IM or email me.
>
> I look forward to hearing from you.
>
> Regards,

My Network –
Little Used Features

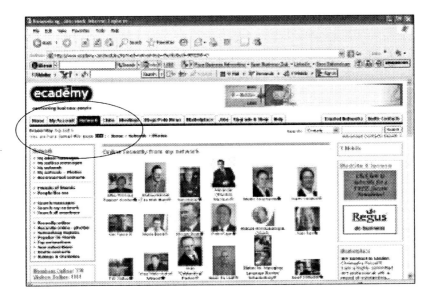

You can also see all the people's photos in your network, and three additional excellent features in the Network section of the site, are:-

Ratings & statistics detailing the world rankings of all members

New Subscribers Gives you a hot list of 100 most recent signups

! If you are in the B2B sector, that link above can be invaluable.

Popular 50 Words the most popular search terms on Ecademy.

! Visit this link, then amend the 50 words in your profile ;)

Clubs

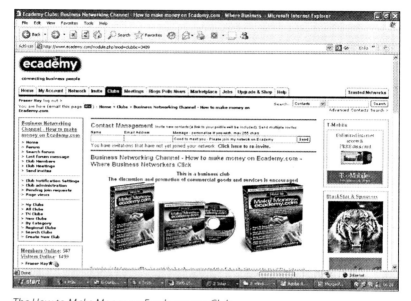

The How to Make Money on Ecademy.com Club

There are over 2000 different clubs on Ecademy with many clubs containing thousands of members. Clubs vary in size, and the seriousness of the topic they cover.

There are hundreds of business clubs, hobby clubs, you name it, and you can also create your own club with a view to building an excellent hot prospect list or opt-in list of people interested in your topic/subject/market sector etc.

Many Ecademy Clubs contain hundreds of members with similar interests, experience, likes and dislikes.

A club is a community of interest where many individuals like to swap and share ideas via a communal forum.

Starting your own club, similar to Blogging, can help position you and your business as an expert or leader in your field and create an opt-in list of prospects or newsletter subscribers very quickly.

There are thousands of clubs to choose from, on everything from website design, to writing a book, to exporting, raising finance to maintaining an optimistic outlook on life. Your Club membership list can grow very quickly, and if you use Marketplace and Blogging as well to promote your club, your membership list could grow to hundreds within a few short months.

If you run your own club, you can choose to set your own rules and code of conduct and whether you will allow members to advertise their own products and services or not. Another interesting feature of a club is the facility to send one email message or promotional offer to all members in your club.

This can be very useful to alert them to a special offer, seasonal promotion or upcoming event.

Read page 134 to find out how to join the How to make Money on Ecademy.com Club for FREE. (RRP £249)

http://www.ecademy.com/module.php?mod=club&c=3489

Personal Meetings

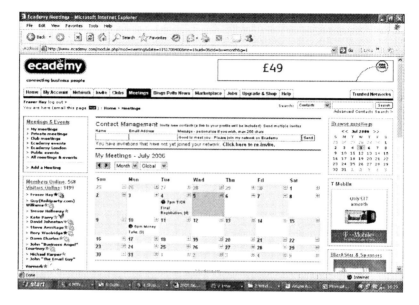

The Meetings section of Ecademy, is excellent for just that.

You can plan future meetings with your fellow ecademists, and the system will even remind you prior to the event as well. All in all, an excellent calendar & reminder system.

How to get speaking engagements

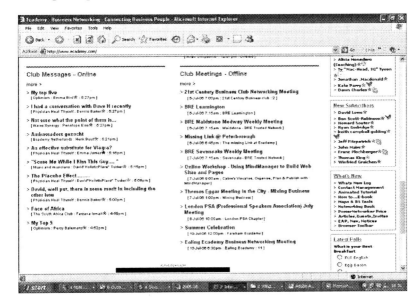

Another excellent feature on the home page of Ecademy is an up-to-date list of all the latest online meetings and regional offline meetings in your area. Here you can find out when to hook up or meet up with other people with similar likes, interests or hobbies.

Alternatively you can also attend a group meeting in your area or nearest town and meet others over a business breakfast, lunch or evening networking event. Regional Ecademy networking events can also be an excellent opportunity for you to raise your profile and offer your services as a speaker at one of these events.

If you'd like the opportunity to speak at such an event, then check out Phil Calvert's 'Ecademy Speakers club' at http://www.ecademy.com/module.php?mod=club&c=1869

Blogs

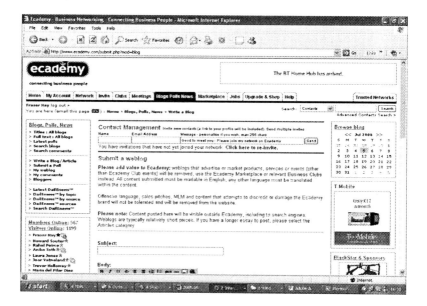

Writing a Blog is an excellent way of raising your profile, awareness, and positioning yourself as an expert in your field of endeavour.

A Blog is an article or message directed to a particular audience that invites participation from others.

Your Blog should be relevant and interesting to your target audience.

By asking questions in your Blog, you invite others to contribute, and the more contribution you have from others, the wider and more frequent your blogs will be read.

By making your Blogs topical or refer to a news item, this can encourage many people to both read and participate in your Blog. A Blog can be an excellent way to get advice, opinions, or help from other people operating in the same industry or area of expertise as yourself. Blogging can be an excellent way of offering advice to others, and position yourself as an expert on a particular topic, subject or theme.

One good thing about Blogging, is that your Blogs are picked up and spidered by Google.com, helping you to get wider awareness for your name or website. Try not to make your Blog too much of a sales pitch, and save or restrict any sales message to the Signature in your Blog. (Please refer to p90 on how to create a profile signature)

One of the fastest ways to get your site found on the internet, is to host a Blog on your website, and promote your blog, by PINGING it or notifying other search engines, directories & news feeds that your blog has been updated.

For a FREE Audio Seminar on Blogging, please go to
http://www.leadgenerationmba.com/How_to_Blog.htm

or alternatively, for details on how to set up a Blog on your website, then please visit:
http://www.ecademy.com/node.php?id=64433

But my favourite blog generating over 1100 views in 48 hrs
http://www.ecademy.com/node.php?id=65746

Marketplace

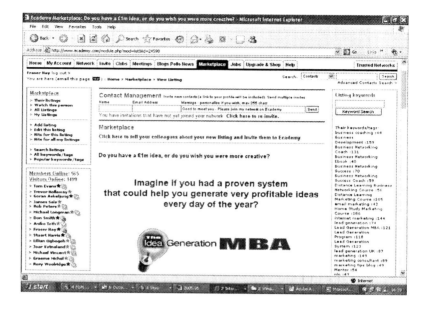

Different ads on Ecademy Marketplace do yield different results, but one of the most important points is to TEST, then TEST again, and then do some more TESTing.

You can test lots of different components of your Marketplace ads. I've tried this on several occasions, and can generate completely different results on occasion, each time a different component is tested.

On the following pages, I've detailed some of my findings, and also the responses to some of my ads.

1. Test Different Objectives

Question why are you placing the ad in the first place. Is it to generate sales, and get people to give you their credit card number? Is the purpose of your ad to raise awareness of what you do? Is the purpose of the ad to point people to your site, and direct traffic to your site, and let it do the selling? Is the purpose of your ad to introduce yourself to your target audience/market, and simply make them aware of your service?. Is it a one stage ad, a two stage ad or a three stage ad. Do you simply want people to visit your profile. Think about it.

2. Test the headline.
Does your headline generate curiosity in the mind of your fellow ecademists? Does your headline make them want to read more, or view the ad? Is the headline relevant to them, and if they read further will they be able to find a solution to their problems, or an answer to the question that you pose in your headline. Are they, and will they be mildly curious in wanting to find out more. Also remember the headline in your Market Place ad is also getting spidered by Google, and may appear on Google in a matter of hours, not days.

3. Test the opening line and sales copy
If they've opened your ad. Are they wanting to read on. What's the compelling reason to read further?

Test the "opening line", and encourage your reader to read on, by generating their interest.

Feedback on ecademy tells me, that people don't like long ads. But offline in direct mail, I subscribe to the "more you tell, the more you sell" school of thought. So keep your ad short, and include links to your main sales tools, presentations, pitches, offers etc like your profile, your website to do the selling, or offer to send them an information pack, or encourage them to contact you to get into dialogue … Remember No. 1 – What's the objective of the ad.

4. Test the inclusion of testimonials and linking to your profile
People tend to want to know more about you before they progress to the next stage in the process. Test putting a link

to your ecademy profile, or a link to the testimonals in your profile. Test Putting a link to your website, your blog, your club. Ecademy is a big community, everybody knows somebody, and testimonials help illustrate the type of advice, quality of service, and what kind of person you are, and the type of organisation or individual you can help.

5. Test different features and benefits
What can you offer the reader. Tell them about the features and the benefits of your products and/or services. Test different benefits to be included in your ad copy. Try including features, or no features - Benefits or no Benefits.

Marketplace is one of the most effective, astounding adver-tising and promotional systems on the internet. There are very few advertising mediums that allow you test every aspect and component of your advert IMMEDIATELY.

Think about this —

If you place an ad in the Yellow Pages, you have to wait a year before you can tell whether it worked or not, and an average ad is about £1500 +.

If you place an ad in your local Chamber of Commerce news-letter, you probably have to wait a month, to see if it worked or not, and an average ad is about £400.

If you place an ad, in your local weekly newspaper, you will have to wait a week to see what the response is like, and then decide which parts of the ad you want to change, at an average cost of £250 per insertion.

If you conduct a mailshot, find the list, print the letter, stuff the 1000 envelopes, then once again, you're going to have to wait about a week, before you can assess whether the mailing was a success, and start the whole process again before you can test different components of your mailing.

Ecademy Marketplace is an incredibly efficient advertising platform, that gives you, the advertiser full control over every aspect of your advert, the targeting of your advert, and the ability to change and test different components of your ad immediately when you decide to.

Ecademy Marketplace ads headlines, and tagging are also spidred by Google, thus allowing your ads to target an even wider audience. This alone is very very powerful, and can save you £££s in online marketing consultancy fees

6. Test Different Pictures.
Have you included a photograph or an image of you, your product, your service in action. Have you tested which pulls best, an image you've uploaded, or an image you're linking to on your profile or on your website. Does your logo outpull a photograph?

People like to see what they're buying, or whats on offer. Show them. Same applies to your profile, if you haven't done so already.

7. Test the offer
Have you tested different offers for the same product or service. Different price points. Have you tested packaging the product with a service, adding more value to your offer. Do you offer a FREE trial of your product, a FREE sample, a FREE consultation, a FREE subscription, a FREE download, are you offering more added value in this offer, than your usual offering.

Are you "selling off the page", or directing people to the sales page on your website?

Are you building your list, and rewarding prospects merely for responding?

8. Test the Deadline
How soon do you want people to respond? Test different dead-

lines. Insert a deadline that your offer runs out. Is it midnight tonight? 24 hours? A week? The end of the month, or there will be an imminent price increase. Test different deadlines, or whether to include them at all.

9. Test the time of day you place your marketplace ad

Some people login to ecademy first thing in the morning. They want the news, the gossip, and want to find out whats happening. Are they ready to buy your product or service?

Maybe. Maybe not. But if they do read your ad and they go out to their meetings, and someone happens to mention they have a requirement for a product or service like yours, and your fellow ecademist remembers your ad, and recommends you, then you may have achieved the objective for your ad.

Some people login to ecademy throughout the day. Same logic applies.

Some people login to ecademy at the end of the day, early evening, mid evening, and late at night. Different audiences have different tastes, and will respond to different offers, and different value based propositions, at different times of the day.

Don't forget its an international online community with different time zones, people will respond to your ad while your sleeping. Imagine that, responses to your marketing while you're sleeping.

10. Test the Call to action and follow up approach.

Once the reader has been intrigued enough to open your ad, having read your headline, read your sales copy, is interested in the offer you present, then consider what you want them to do next.

Do you want them to EMAIL you, TELEPHONE you, MESSAGE you, SKYPE you etc. Tell them exactly what to do next.

Remember people communicate one of 3 ways - visually, audi-tory, kinesthetically.

Consider other people's preferred mode of communication, and let them choose their preferred method to respond. Give them options.

If you want them to visit your profile to get your phone number – tell them.

If you want them to visit your profile to get your email address – tell them.

If you want them to visit your profile to send you a message – tell them.

If you want them to visit your website – tell them.

Don't leave them wondering, what to do next.

Last but not least – Follow up.
If you get given a business card or if you give someone a busi-ness card, at a networking event, what do you tend to do? You follow up.

If you get a response from your ad in the press, and they don't buy first time, what do you do? You follow up.

If you collect business cards and enquiries from the recent trade fair you attended, what do you do? You follow up.

If you get a response via your website, and they don't buy first time, what do you do? You follow up.

THE SAME APPLIES TO YOUR MARKETPLACE ADS.

For if they are not interested – they will very soon tell you.

At the time of writing I've only been on Ecademy 8 months, and keep finding something new – tools/resources and features here on Ecademy to try, to test, to explore, and to integrate into my marketing approach, but one thing's for sure – they do work, and are highly beneficial – if you use them consistently.

When you check the response to your ads, if an individual has clicked on your ad more than once in the same day, then it's indicative that they are interested in what you do. Also check the time that they responded, and the length of time they spent reading your ad/profile, and the gap between the times.

Actual Responses to Headlines Tested

- Do you offer consultancy, coaching or management advice? 153 views
- Want to work with me & allow me to earn revenue for both of us? 209 views
- FREE Marketing Strategy Advice for 2006. 240 views
- How to ensure you and your business profit from Ecademy. 256 views
- How to Make Money on Ecademy.com. 371 views

Assuming the reader is on the home page, the next step is to get their attention. If your headline doesn't catch their attention you can kiss your response and sales goodbye. People have a very short attention span and if your headline doesn't attract their attention and peek their interest, they will just not click on the link and view your ad. But the real secret to generating sales via Marketplace is not in the people who view your ads, its in the number of people you convert by following up.

Conversions of up to 5-10% or more, are not unusual, but it can take up to 4/5 contacts/follow ups to get into dialogue, develop trust and achieve your objective. That's the secret.

Even more case studies, results and recommendations in the How to Make Money on Ecademy.com Club. Check it out.

http://www.ecademy.com/module.php?mod=club&c=3489

How to Guarantee Your Ads Get Found

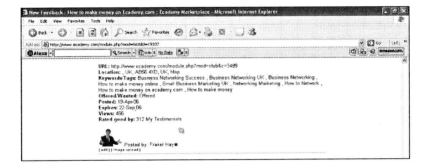

Don't forget about your Keyword Tags. The keywords you use to help get your ads found on Ecademy, can also help to get your ads published and found on Google.com often within 2 hours of the ad appearing on ecademy.com.

Don't forget to follow up those people who read your ads. They were interested enough to view your Market Place ad, so follow them up. Your ad might have appeared at one time of day, and since disappeared off the home page. Your follow up email, might be sent at a time of day, better suited for them to reply, it may have jogged their memory and politely reminded them, maybe not. But you won't know unless you follow up and ask.

For a FREE Audio Seminar on Marketplace, go to:
http://www.leadgenerationmba.com/marketplace_intro.htm

What I have learnt so far:

Getting Found on Google.com

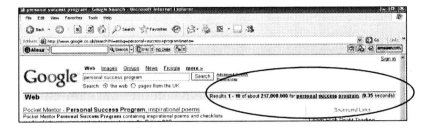

With the help of Ecademy, I beat 200,000,000* sites to get the first 3 positions on Google

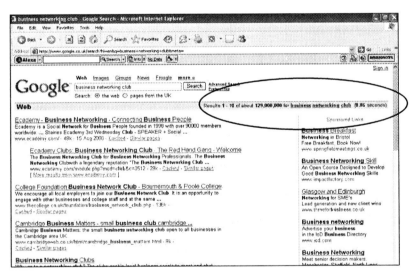

With the help of Ecademy, I beat 120,000,000* sites for a Page 1 listing on Google.

*Please note actual rankings can fluctuate, and need to be regularly maintained

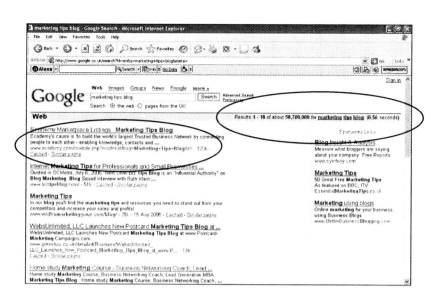

Four Weeks from INCEPTION, my marketing tips blog is found on page one on Google beating 50,000,000 other sites

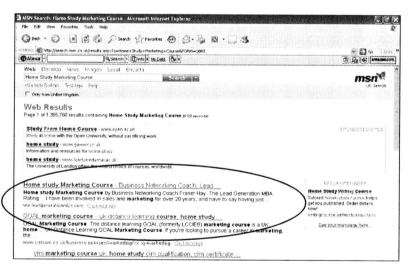

Positions #1 on MSN.com for Home Study Marketing Course

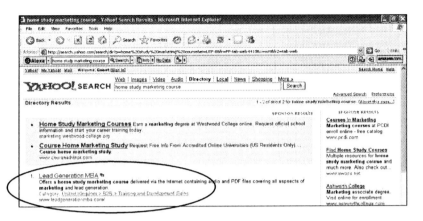

Position #1 on Yahoo.com for Home Study Marketing Course

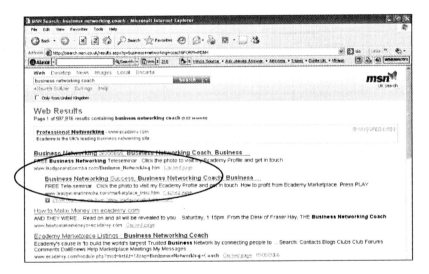

Occupying first few slots on MSN for 'business networking coach'.

*Please note actual rankings can fluctuate, and need to be regularly maintained.

Ecademy has an excellent link popularity on the major search engines, and by tweaking your profile & Marketplace ads on Marketplace it can greatly assist you in your search engine rankings, saving you hundreds of ££££s per annum.

Generate a reputation for Customer Care that's not just the best ... BUT LEGENDARY

Here are some excellent guidelines on good customer care, when dealing with new contacts on Ecademy.com. And an excellent taster for some of the additional things I've learned during my journey on Ecademy.com

1. Keep a promise

As an ecademist, you'll win business by promising service and will retain business by keeping this promise. Keeping to a promise is such a basic test that it is both surprising and frustrating that so many people fail to do it.

If you promise to send information to a Prospect within 48 hours, then do so.

If you promise to reply to a question in writing, by a particular time then do so.

If you promise to call back this evening, then do so.

Provide a fast, efficient and friendly service and prove it with a charm, and courtesy that is earning Ecademy a legendary reputation.

> **Ecademy Tip:** The more promises you make and keep, the better the service, the faster your reputation and network will grow.

2. Ten second telephone response and 15 second website loading time response

Consumers are becoming more demanding today than ever before. They do vary. Prospects and customers have thresholds. But one thing EVERY prospect or customer hates is a telephone that continues to ring without being answered, especially when they are the one dialling the number. There's no excuse, an effective telephone response must always be a priority - even if its just an answer machine with a recorded message, your virtual switchboard, or voicemail. Ensure that you or your "answering service" answer all incoming telephone calls.

If you don't - you will lose opportunities and sales. Always include your telephone number in an ad, emails and your profile (not everyone has heard of SKYPE).

Same could also be said for a webpage that takes ages to load. People are impatient, and can quickly lose interest. Not everyone who visits your website has broadband. Make your profile interesting, relevant, and easy for people to contact you.

> **Ecademy Tip:** Your Profile on Ecademy can often be the FIRST and the LAST point of contact a prospect/customer will have with you.
>
> The telephone is often the FIRST and the LAST point of contact a prospect/customer will have with you.
>
> Your Website can often be the FIRST and the LAST point of contact a prospect/customer will have with you.
>
> Make an impact and be professional

3. Fast "information" requests within 24 hours

Any "request for information" should be actioned immediately, or at the very least same day. There can be no excuses, not with the power of internet, Personal Messaging, MSN Messenger, fax machines, webcasting, SKYPE and couriers.

You can direct people to your website, or you can offer to send them the information by post, or at the very least – you could offer to send them the information by email.

This also applies not just to the initial contact, but also requests for information, brochureware, answers to questions.

Think about the different types of requests for information you can have to your ads, emails, mailings and communications …

* The method of response
* The speed of the response
* The quality of the response
* Who will respond.

Ecademy Tip: A quick courteous response saves time, creates goodwill and is 1000% more profitable than any delay

---

4. Positive attitude

Every single interaction between a prospect, customer or partner and you should be conducted in a courteous, friendly, and positive way with a genuine and interested focus on them.

Granted some people can and do behave in an atrocious manner, but this is a very small minority and simply does not represent the 99% majority.

Funnily enough, it doesn't actually take much to please most prospects and customers. Conversely, it doesn't take much to alienate people either. Customers can be extraordinarily forgiving if not extraordinarily appreciative of any positive attitude displayed by you.

One of the best ways to generate a positive attitude is to adopt the right mindset or write your own elevator pitch and USP and memorise it. You should also write your own personal list of facts, features and benefits of what you like about your product or service and what makes it different.

> **Ecademy Tip:** A positive attitude must always emanate from you all the time you are speaking with prospects, networking contacts & customers. Ooze enthusiasm. (and remember the last four letters of enthusIASM - I Am Sold Myself. (You do what you do, because you believe in it with a passion)

5. Become a happeneur - be proactive
When things go wrong (and they sometimes do), try and get to the customer before the customer gets to you. Things will go wrong. Sometimes it is outside of your control or influence. Whatever happens, it is imperative that you are proactive.

By being proactive, you will create goodwill by contacting customers about problems before they find out about them some other way. Same applies to your prospecting, and networking, remember faint heart never won fair maiden.

> **Ecademy Tip:** When the customer reacts, it's often too late, far better that you speak first and take action accordingly. You have to kiss a lot of frogs, before you find your prince.

6. Honesty and openness
All of your emails, phone calls, and other communications must be of a completely open and honest basis. Nothing should be hidden from the customer. Granted, it can be a struggle to tell the truth when things go wrong, especially when there has been a high degree of incompetence, or miscommunication,

resulting in a massive inconvenience to a customer. But tell the truth, it will always pay off. People understand that things can go wrong on occasion, so always tell the truth.

Some common things that can go wrong:

A prospect's postal address or email address can be incorrectly recorded

Your server could be down for maintenance (very rarely, most guarantee 99% up time)

Due to the volume of enquiries and current work load, there is a short delay or you simply forgot.

Honesty and openness also relate to those all important details of customer service, like a promise to call back, put answers to questions, or cc a contact in a personal message, or send a document by email or in the post. Everything you say to your prospects and customers must be on an open and honest basis.

> **Ecademy Tip:** If you confirm everything in writing to your prospect/customer – then there can be no misunderstandings. (This can be done by email, by post, by fax, or by Personal Message).

7. Systems reliability
Your service system, should fail the customer on no more than one in a hundred occasions.

As mentioned in 6 on page 119, Endeavour to maintain a 99% uptime with your computer servers, and the majority of cases all your customers will feel that everything is under control, that everything works, and when something occasionally does go wrong, the problem is identified and is fixed quickly and efficiently.

System reliability also relates to the system or process that you use to respond, sell or educate prospects and customers. The system works, you just have to ensure that you use it, manage it well in addition to your time and promotional spend.

> **Ecademy Tip:** A systems failure, is no more than a management failure. Often it's not the failure that's important, but how you react to it, that it is.

8. Action speaks volumes

Immediate action must be taken, without hesitation to redress any shortfall in service to your customer. We have mentioned earlier, that sometimes things can go wrong that can be outside of "our" control, and we do on occasion have to tolerate the imperfections of our fellow human beings. What can be intolerable is the 'second order' failure to make swift reparation to the 'first order' reparation. Most of us will tolerate a mistake if it is openly and honestly admitted and early action is taken to redress it.

Things can and will go wrong - it is inevitable, but the key test here is that you take remedial action to solve any customer problem as they happen upon you.

> **Ecademy Tip:** See number 6 on page 119

9. Being in the Know. Ecademists should be in the ' KNOW ':

- Know your product / service
- Know your promotional and sales process
- Know how to get things done
- Know who to speak to, to get problems resolved on Ecademy
- Know how well you are progressing

Ignorance is far form bliss when the customer fails to get an answer, fails to receive sensible advice or fails to elicit a meaningful response.

As an ecademist there are a number of ways to help you become in the 'know ':-

- Refer to a buddy or mentor on Ecademy.com
- Refer to the blogging section of the home page and ask your fellow ecademists for help
- Refer to one of the specific clubs here on ecademy
- Place a wanted ad on Marketplace Email Support

Ecademy Tip: The only way your customers can know that you are the best, is when you are in the ' know '

---

10. Who's in the Firing Line?

The person who interfaces directly with a customer in your business, must be able and willing to respond effectively to a customer and therefore have the discretion to make a decision in that customer's favour, whatever the circumstance.

There's nothing more frustrating than the sorts of response that go like this:

'Sorry I can't help you, let me speak to …'

'That person is on holiday, I'll have to speak to … about this.'

'It's got nothing to do with me, you'd better ask …'

As soon as you start 'shunting' problems back to customer, and not taking ownership or responsibility for them, your customers will lose patience, and you will lose sales.

You are responsible for dealing with your customers.

> **Ecademy Tip:** Customers "contract" with you. You contract with your suppliers and partners. If you need help and assistance, please also see number 9 on page 123 for help.

11. Little Extras

Customer expectations should frequently be exceeded by the provision of unsolicited little extras.

As an Ecademist, you should take delight in pleasing your customers. In itself, the basic product; or service provided by you, and purchased by the customer might not always be pleasurable. What should be pleasurable, is when the customer receives something good and above what is expected.

> **Ecademy Tip:** Little extras cost very little – and the difference between ordinary and extraordinary, is that little extra.

12. Crossing the T's and Dotting the i's

The fine detail of customer service should always be near to perfect. Pareto's Principle applies here. 80% of customer dissatisfaction comes from getting 20% of the detail wrong

If someone asks for the information to be emailed to them and not posted - email it.

Ensure you spell people's name correctly

If you state a time in your ad, when to call - ensure you are in and able to receive the calls

We all lead busy lives, but it is our attention to detail that really distinguishes a really superb business professional from a poor one.

By getting the detail right, you ensure you get everything else right too. 'Getting it right' is not what you say and do, but also HOW you do it. Admittedly, everyone can miss some detail, so no-one is perfect.

> **Ecademy Tip:** Attention to detail is the ultimate test of a really caring professional attitude towards your customers

http://www.leadgenerationmba.com/

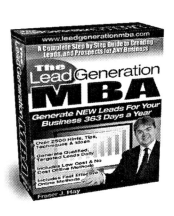

Ecademy Jobs

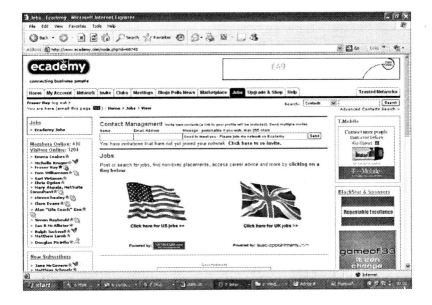

If you're looking for a job then Ecademy.com has hundreds of vacancies advertising senior positions from major executive recruiters and employers across the UK, Europe and the rest of the world. In addition to permanent, interim and contract opportunities, Ecademy also advertises non-executive, trustee & senior voluntary roles.

Employers can also advertise to reach thousands of talented and highly-qualified executives. Create your own high-quality display ad online and start receiving responses in hours.

Upgrading Your Membership

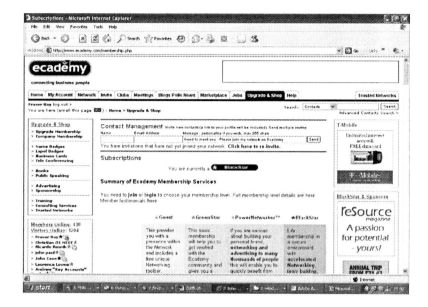

For more information on the membership options, please visit the following url on Ecademy.com

www.ecademy.com/account.php?op=signup&xref=90022

Getting Help when you need it

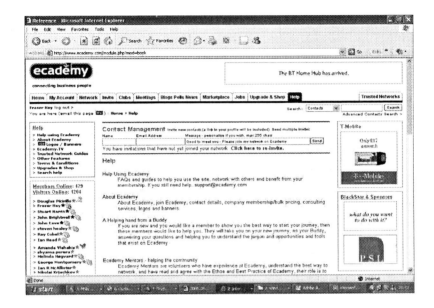

Help Using Ecademy
http://www.ecademy.com/node.php?id=44

About Ecademy
http://www.ecademy.com/node.php?id=315

Helping Hand from a Buddy
http://www.ecademy.com/node.php?id=58772

Ecademy Mentors – helping the Community
http://www.ecademy.com/node.php?id=59994

The Ultimate Resource on Ecademy:
http://www.ecademy.com/module.php?mod=club&c=3512

How to Guarantee Your Future Success

1. Do you recall the 7 fundamentals of Ecademy? Yes/No
2. Have you evaluated your last 12 months? Yes/No
3. Have you studied your daily thoughts for Ecademy? Yes/No
4. Have you planned your Time/Set your goals? Yes/No
5. Have you created a profile on Ecademy? Yes/No
6. Have you reviewed your photo, 50 words and voice tag? Yes/No
7. Have you linked to your website/listed benefits/skills? Yes/No
8. Have you reviewed the signature on your profile? Yes/No
9. Have you asked for testimonials for your profile yet? Yes/No
10. Does your profile contain google spidered keywords? Yes/No
11. Have you followed up your profile hits on a daily basis? Yes/No
12. Have you followed up/welcomed NEW Subscribers? Yes/No
13. Have you created /joined/contributed to a club yet? Yes/No
14. Have you planned your meetings for this month? Yes/No
15. Have you written or contributed to a blog yet? Yes/No
16. Have you placed an ad on Marketplace yet? Yes/No
17. Have you attended a regional event/club yet? Yes/No
18. Have your marketplace ads been found on Google yet? Yes/No

19. Have you practiced good customer service ethics?   Yes/No

20. Have you upgraded to Power Networker/
    BlackStar yet?   Yes/No

21. Have you taken advantage of the 50% discount
    voucher yet on page 134?   Yes/No

If you answer No to any of the questions, please refer to the
appropriate section in part 2 of the book (& repeat 3-19 often

How can I personally help you?

Would you (or any of your contacts) like help, assistance, or advice for:

- Targeting prospective clients, who are most likely in need of your product or service?
- Persuasively communicate how your products/services fill their needs?
- Do you want help in converting the maximum no. of prospective clients into new customers?
- Convert first-time buyers to repeat customers?
- I may also be able to introduce you to some of my contacts, Create new additional strategic relationships, JVs and new opportunities for **your business**

For some of the comments from other ecademists, details of the awards that I've won, or some of the accomplishments I've achieved over the years, and details of **how I can help you**, then get in touch below.

http://www.ecademy.com/account.php?id=90022&xref=90022

The Lead Generation MBA

- 18 Sessions, totalling over 9 hours of audio
- Over 2500 different techniques, concepts, strategies and ideas for increasing revenue
- Ideal for Businesses in the Retail, Wholesale, Manufacturing & Professional Services sectors
- Now containing techniques & concepts for over 625 different market segments, industries & Niches
- Covers Online and Offline techniques for every kind of budget (even those on a shoestring)
- Complete with Prospect Tracking System to ensure 100% of Sales Opportunities are never lost
- Live 1-2-1 Mentoring Support
- Live Group Teleconference Sessions
- Personalised Live 1-2-1 Ecademy Help to maximise your Ecademy Experience & ROI
- Generous Discounts for Ecademy Members off the RRP

For FREE sample session from our Home Study Marketing Course, visit:
http://www.leadgenerationmba.com

POCKET Mentor™

Master your thoughts and transform your life with the **Pocket Mentor**™; the internationally acclaimed diary based self improvement and achievement system that guarantees results.

Combining motivational and inspirational quotations, poems, anecdotes and checklists all integrated into one unique simple to use system, **Pocket Mentor**™ will motivate and inspire you into action. The catalyst of positive change, **Pocket Mentor**™ is a proven, powerful self improvement and achievement system

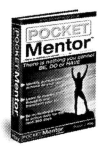

"Quite simply, this is one of the most profound, effective, and value for money, personal development tools on the market today. The ingenious combination of inspirational poems, inspirational quotes, sayings, anecdotes and checklists cleverly integrated into one complete self help diary based system is exceptional. Whether you are an athlete, a business professional, in full time education, a parent or simply at a crossroads in your life, this powerful and unique system will help you to boost your self esteem, find clarity, focus and direction and achieve the results you crave"

Dr. Michael de La Mothe, C.Psychol, AFBPsS

www.pocketmentor.co.uk

FREE Audio Seminars

FREE Personal Success Seminar

The Four Step Formula for Success

FREE personal development Seminar -

How to Think for Success

FREE personal success Seminar -

How to Make Money on Ecademy.com with MarketPlace

FREE Online Marketing Seminar -

How to Succeed at Blogging on Ecademy.com

FREE networking Seminar

How to Succeed at Business Card Marketing

FREE Personal Marketing Seminar

How to Succeed on Ecademy.com as a Power Networker

FREE Lead Generation Seminar

The 10 Commandments of Lead Generation

FREE Online Marketing Seminar

How to Generate Leads by writing articles & E-books

FREE Life Coaching Seminar

Complete with Handouts

All of the above seminars can also be accessed

via my profile on Ecademy.com

http://www.ecademy.com/account.php?id=90022&xref=90022

As a thank you for purchasing my book, please accept this Gift Certificate with my compliments.

£249 Gift Certificate

I hereby confirm that
The recipient of this voucher
is entitled to a £249 discount
off the following products:

Lead Generation MBA RRP £997, Special Price £748
1 Year Club Subscription RRP £249, Special Price £FREE

The above gift certificate entitles the customer to a **£249** discount on either of the above listed products. This Certificate can only be used once, but you never know, I might just be in a good mood, the day you call me to "cash it in".

Please quote Your Ecademy.com Profile ID and Book Purchase receipt No. when ordering. Contact me Below.

http://www.ecademy.com/account.php?id=90022&xref=90022

Welcome to Business Networking ("on steroids")

The Red Hand Gang

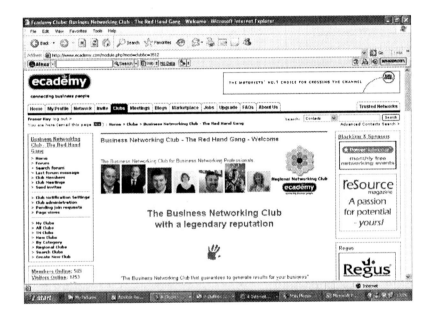

http://www.ecademy.com/module.php?mod=club&c=3512

THE ULTIMATE BUSINESS NETWORKING RESOURCE

Printed in the United Kingdom
by Lightning Source UK Ltd.
115277UKS00001B/271-279